Cedronio

**A Pocket Guide for Travellers at Naples by E. Cedronio Traslated from the French and Revised by J. M**

Cedronio

**A Pocket Guide for Travellers at Naples by E. Cedronio Traslated from the French and Revised by J. M**

ISBN/EAN: 9783741149832

Manufactured in Europe, USA, Canada, Australia, Japa

Cover: Foto ©Andreas Hilbeck / pixelio.de

Manufactured and distributed by brebook publishing software (www.brebook.com)

Cedronio

# A Pocket Guide for Travellers at Naples by E. Cedronio Traslated from the French and Revised by J. M

# A POCKET GUIDE

FOR

## TRAVELLERS AT NAPLES

BY

### E. CEDRONIO

Translated from the french and revised

BY J. M.

NAPLES
PRINTED BY GIANNINI
Via Museo Nazionale 31.
1872

## A FEW PREFATORY WORDS

*The pocket Guide is not intended to replace those voluminous and often embarrassing works in which one finds the minute and detailed description of all that a town contains. But as simple « Vade-Mecum » its practical aim and immediate use limits itself to furnishing the traveller arriving at Naples, for the first time, with the necessary hints for his comfort in lodging and board, and show him those excursions considered indispensable whatever be the length of his stay.*

*A list of well-chosen addresses will also show the traveller where to buy at reasonable prices, all that this town offers in objects of art and local industry.*

# INTRODUCTION

The town of Naples, on the bay of the same name, is situaded at 40° 52' north latitude, and 11° 55' 45" east of Paris. Its soil is of a volcanic constitution, its ordinary temperature from 13 to 14 degrees Reaumur. The greatest heat is about 26 degrees, its maximum of cold from 1 to 2 degrees below zero.

Naples, seen from the sea, has the appearance of an amphitheatre reflected again in the clear blue waters of its bay. The verdant hills surrounding it are dotted with pretty villas. The whole panorama is bright and picturesque and is the admiration of all who arrive on its hospitable shores.

The inhabitants are of a lively and happy disposition, and have a decided taste for singing and music.

The origin of Naples is lost in tradition of the greatest antiquity. It was first called *Phalère*, and then was given the name of the Syren Parthenope.

Envious of its prosperity and delightful situation, the people of Cumae destroyed it. Some time after, an epidemic desolating their town, the Cumeans consulted their Sibyl on the means of appeasing the gods; they ordered them to rebuild the city they had destroyed, and to establish there the worship of Parthenope, which they did in the hope of deliverance from their scourge.

The new buildings were not raised exactly on the site of the old town, though that also was partly rebuilt, and the result was that two towns appeared side by side. It was then to distinguish them that the name of Palaepolis, or old town, was given to the one, and that of Neapolis, or new town, to the other. Soon after these two made only one, Neapolis.

It is useless to weary the reader with the changes which accompany the long existence of this interesting city. However it would be worthwhile remarking that its position so favourable to commerce, the fertility of its soil, and the mildness of its climate constantly excited the cupidity of all European nations. After being a Roman colony until the fall of the empire it became the prey of the Barbarians. Rescued from these it was governed, more than a century, by foreign dukes; then in turn ruled by the emperors of the east, and those of Germany. At the commencement of the twelfth century, the Normans took it from them, Roger, their chief, already master of the Puglie, the Calabrias, and of Sicily, converted these many territories ( about the year 1130 ) into one single state to which he gave a legislative constitution. Naples then became one of the seats of this combination. The imperial house of Hoenstaufen succeeded the Normans by right of heritage, then the Angevins by right of conquest. After these the Durazzo, the Aragonesi, the Spaniards and the Austrians ruled this country alternately until the accession of Charles 3$^{rd}$ of the dynasty of the Spanish Bourbons, after his victory at Bitonto over the Imperialists in 1734.

We should require more space than

we can give in this short notice, to mention all the material reminders left by those various foreign rulers.

Wishing to limit ourselves only to speaking of those which may help us to link together the historical periods we have slightly sketched, we will say that the Normans built the Castle Capuano, now a *Court of Justice* and prison ; the celebrated Frederick 2nd, about the beginning of the 13.[th] century founded the University ; the Angevins raised the Castel Nuovo, the Cathedral, and the Certosa of S.' Martino, and to the viceroys of Spain are owed the street of Toledo and the edifice of the national Museum. Of all the conquerors only one identified himself with his new country; this was Charles the 3rd. His reign marks for Naples a new era of prosperity and grandeur, by wisdom in administration by useful reforms and by the construction of noble buildings, such as the royal palace of Caserta and that of Capodimonte, the theatre of S.' Carlo, the large Asylum for the poor etc. etc.

The reign of the Bourbons was interrupted by the republic (1799) and by the monarchies of Joseph Bonaparte and Joachim Murat (1806 to 1815).

In 1860 the month of May Garibaldi landed at Marsala in Sicily with a thousand volunteers, gained possession of the Island already in a state of revolution against the Bourbon; then crossed to the continent dispersed the army of the latter in the other meridional provinces of his kingdom, and arrived at Naples the $7^{th}$ of September of the same year. The Neapolitans received him with enthusiastic joy and masters of their destiny by the Plebiscite of the $21^{st}$ of Octobre of the following month sealed their union to the rest of Italy under the sceptre of Victor Emanuel $2^{nd}$. At the present time Naples is no more than the mere chief town of a province of that name with a prefecture and a military command; not the less does it retain its importance and brightness. The population is about 600000 inhabitants.

# FIRST PART

**Arrival at Naples.** — Every traveller arriving at Naples whether by land or sea is subjected to the examination of his luggage as the only formality he has to fulfil.

We commence therefore by giving the tariff of the boats, the carriage of luggage, and the hired carriages.

## BOATS

Every traveller coming from foreign ports, from those of North Italy and Sicily with or without luggage . Fr. (*Lira italiana*) 1,00
From the gulf of Gaeta or Salerno . 0,40
From the islands of Ischia, Procida, Capri, or other points of the bay of Naples . . . . . . . . . . . . . 0,20

NOTE. — *Children under five years old are free. From five to twelve half price, and over twelve full price.*

## Transport of luggage

*From the quay to the carriage.*
For one or more trunks of which the weight does not exceed 100 hilos . . . Fr. 0,40
For the same from 100 Kilos to 200 » 0,60
*From the bureau to the exit from the station, and* vice-versa.
For one trunk not above 100 Kilos » 0,20
The same from 101 to 200 Kilos » 0,40
Small baggage, bags, hat boxes etc. » 0,10
*Taken to residence from the Port or station.*
For one trunk not above 100 Kilos » 1,00
Idem, from 101 to 200 Kilos . » 1,50

---

**Necessary caution.** *Before giving the tariff for the carriages we warn all travellers they will do well to avoid any discussion with the drivers. In case of a dispute they can call the police or retain the number of the carriage and apply to the central Bureau of the Corso Pubblico at the Hotel de Ville Piazza del Municipio 1.$^{st}$ floor.*

*Strangers are reminded that the Italian money is of the same value as the French and equally divided into decimal fractions.*

# CAB AND CARRIAGE FARES

## One horse cab

### From day break to midnight

|  | F. |  |
|---|---|---|
| The fare . . . . . . . | » | 00 | 60 |
| By the hour — 1st hour . . | » | 1 | 40 |
| The following hours . . | » | 1 | 00 |

### From midnight to day break

|  | F. |  |
|---|---|---|
| The fare . . . . . . . | » | 1 | 00 |
| By the hour — 1st hour . . | » | 2 | 00 |
| The following hours . . | » | 1 | 40 |

## Carriage with two horses

### From day break to midnight

|  | F. |  |
|---|---|---|
| The fare . . . . . . . | » | 1 | 20 |
| By the hour — 1st hour . . | » | 2 | 00 |
| The following hours . . | » | 1 | 50 |

### From midnight to day break

|  | F. |  |
|---|---|---|
| The fare . . . . . . . | » | 1 | 00 |
| By the hour — 1st hour . . | » | 3 | 00 |
| The following hours . . | » | 2 | 00 |

**Limits of the drive**—The Tondo of Capodimonte—The chinese house of the Granili—The Bridge of Casanova—The beginning of the street of St Giovanni e Paolo—The Largo Gesù e Maria—The Fontanelle—The Largo of the St Carlo alle Mortelle—The fountain of the Leone at Mergellina—Largo Piedigrotta.

## FARES OF CARRIAGES OUT OF TOWN

| One horse cab | F. | |
|---|---|---|
| From Naples to Pausilipe | 1 | 50 |
| »   »   to Capodimonte | 1 | 50 |
| »   »   to the Arenella, Antignano, or Vomero | 1 | 50 |
| »   »   to Fuorigrotta | 1 | 20 |
| »   »   Bagnoli or lake of Agnano | 2 | 00 |
| »   »   Miano and Marianella | 2 | 00 |
| »   »   Piscinola | 2 | 50 |
| »   »   Portici | 1 | 75 |
| »   »   S. Giorgio a Cremano | 1 | 75 |
| »   »   Barra | 1 | 75 |
| »   »   Resina | 2 | 00 |
| »   »   Torre del Greco | 2 | 50 |

| Two horse carriage | F. | |
|---|---|---|
| From Naples to Pausilipe | 2 | 25 |
| »   »   to Capodimonte | 2 | 25 |
| »   »   to the Arenella, Antignano, or Vomero | 2 | 25 |
| »   »   to Fuorigrotta | 1 | 75 |
| »   »   Bagnoli or lake of Agnano | 3 | 00 |
| »   »   Miano and Marianella | 3 | 00 |
| »   »   Piscinola | 3 | 75 |
| »   »   Portici | 2 | 50 |
| »   »   S. Giorgio a Cremano | 2 | 50 |
| »   »   Barra | 2 | 50 |
| »   »   Resina | 3 | 00 |
| »   »   Torre del Greco | 3 | 75 |

**Note.** — *The above prices for drives out of Naples are only compulsory if the carriage has been taken at the station nearest the place to which the traveller wishes to go. In all other cases, a little addition, equal to the amount of one fare is the drivers due. The traveller has the right to the carriage of his small baggage, for every trunk 20 centimes extra. These tariffs are invariable.*

**The choice of an hotel** depends chiefly on the means at one's disposal. Naples has Hotels in its most beautiful quarters ( Chiaia and St. Ferdinando) in sight of the bay, and others which, less well situated, are still to be recommended for their comfort and cleanliness. These which are nearer the centre of the town are suitable for business people — Here are some addresses :

*Riviera di Chiaia*
    HÔTEL DE LA GRANDE BRETAGNE N.º 276.
    HÔTEL D' ANGLETERRE N.º 270.
    HÔTEL DU LOUVRE N.º 255, 253.
    HÔTEL DE LA VILLE N.º 127.

*Largo Vittoria*
    HÔTEL VITTORIA.
    HÔTEL DE NAPLES.

*Strada Vittoria*
    GRAND-HÔTEL D' AMERIQUE

*Chiatamone*
    UNITED STATES GRAND HOTEL N.º 7.
    HÔTEL DES ETRANGERS N.º 9.
    HÔTEL WASHINGTON.
    HÔTEL CROCELLE.

*Strada St. Lucia.*
    HÔTEL DE ROME.

Hôtel de Russie N.º 82.
Hôtel de Belle-vue N.º 71.
*Strada Nardones*
   Hôtel Montpellier N.º 8.
   Hôtel d'Europe N.º 118.
*Strada Medina*
   Hôtel Central N.º 72.
*Strada St. Giuseppe*
   Hôtel de Genève N.º 13.
*Via Molo*
   Hôtel Milano N.º 24.
*Largo Fiorentini*
   Hôtel dei Fiori.
*Via Gennaro Serra*
   Hôtel du Plebiscite N. 24.

Several Boarding houses on the Chiaja offer comfortable lodging at relatively moderate prices.

*Riviera di Chiaja*
   Pension Anglo-Americaine N.º 211.
   Succursale N.º 180.
   Pension Anglaise N,º 114.
   Pension de la Riviera N.º 118.
   Pension Suez N.º 36.

*Strada Giovanni Bausan*
    ENGLISH BOARDING-HOUSE N.º 64.
*Strada Santa Teresa a Chiaja*
    PENSION D'EUROPE N.º 10.

After these hints, when the traveller has made choice of an hotel or boarding house, we hope to anticipate his first wishes and wants by giving the addresses of our best bathing establishments.

    Hot and cold bath.— *Via della Pace.*
    Idem— *Vico Belle Donne a Chiaja* N.º 12.
    Idem — *Strada S. Marco a Fontana Medina* N.º 6.
    Idem — Hotel de Rome — *Strada S.$^{ta}$ Lucia.*
    Hydropathic establishment directed by D.$^r$ Fabre — *Largo Ascensione a Chiaia.*
    Idem directed by D.$^r$ Paoni. *Strada Cavallerizza* N.º 47.

---

For all relating to food, at the above named hotels and boarding houses one can have all one wishes; travellers, however, preferring to dine in the town, will find good cooking, and clean attendance, at the following Cafés and Restaurants.

Réstaurant du Nord — Strada Nardones N.º 118.

Réstaurant de la Ville de Naples — Strada St. Brigida N.º 2.

Réstaurant Fils de Pietro—Mergellina.

Café-Réstaurant dell' Italia Meridionale — Strada di Chiaja N.º 83.

*At this little café an excellent and cheap lunch can be obtained.*

Café du Commerce — Fontana Medina (where the cuisine is excessively French).

Café-Réstaurant Suisse — Same street.

Café del Nuovo Mondo — Strada Piliero N.º 27.

Besides two first class café restaurants.

Grand Café du Palais Royal and Café d'Europe — Piazza St. Ferdinando.

---

To these indispensable directions for the moment of arrival, follow those which might be necessary to a traveller during his stay in our town.

General administration poste Office Strada Montoliveto

(*Succursales*) Piazza St. Caterina a Chiaja — Strada Foria N.º 147 — Railway Station — and the. Édifice of the Immaculatella close to the port

. TELEGRAPHS — Central office, Strada Montoliveto.

(*Succursales*) Strada St. Teresa à Chiaja 6.
Strada S. Giacomo N.º 42.
Strada Foria N.º 108.

BANKERS.

DE GAZ and sons — Strada Trinità Maggiore N.º 53.

MEURICOFFRE AND C.º — Piazza of the Municipe N.º 52.

ROGERS AND BROTHERS — Piazza of the Municipe N.º 52.

W. J. TURNER AND C.º — Strada St. Lucia N.º 64.

IGGULDEN AND C.º — Riviera di Chiaja at the entrance of the Villa garden.

BANCA ANGLO-ITELIENNE — Vico Campane a Toledo N.º 33.

FÉRAUD, AND SONS — Strada Nardones N.º 8.

BANCA ITALO-GERMANICA, Strada di Chiaia N.º 37.

Cerulli et C.º 29 Vittoria.

ENGLISH AND AMERICAN BANK—Riviera di Chiaja N.º 267.

### Consular agents

France — Via Poerio N.º 34.
England — Montoliveto N.º 70.
Austria — Strada S. Giacomo N.º 29.
Russia — Via Poerio N.º 34.
Germany — Fontana Medina N.º 47.
Spain — Strada Fiorentini N.º 5.
Belgium — Strada Donnalbina N.º 56.
Holland — Piazza del Municipio N.º 52.
Principality of Monaco—Strada della Pace
Denmark — Vico 1.º Piliero N.º 1.
République of S. Marino — Vico Carogiojello N.º 15.
Portugal — Toledo N.º 329.
Tunis — Strada St. Marco N.º 4.
Greece — Via Poerio N.º 34.
Turkey — Riviera di Chiaja N.º 48.
United States — Piazza del Municipio N.º 52.
Colombia — Strada dei Pellegrini N.º 19.
New Granada — Porta Medina N.º 49.
République of Guatimala — Largo Mondragone N.º 3.
République of Salvador — Toledo Nº 185.

République Argentine — Piazza del Municipio N.º 52.
Bresil — Strada Toledo N.º 424.
Bolivia — Strada Costantinopoli N.º 30.
Perù — Pizzo-falcone N.º 73.
Chilì — St. Giacomo N.º 29.
Costa-Ricca — Fontana Medina N.º 5.
Equador — Strada S. Pasquale à Chiaja N.º 19.
Mexico — Porta Medina N.º 49.
Republic of Uraguay — Via Gennaro Serra N.º 69.
Persia — Piazza del Municipio N.º 8.
Republic of Honduras — Strada della Pace N.º 27.

POLICE OFFICE (Questura) — Strada Concezione a Toledo.

**Libraries also for subscribers.**

DETKEN AND ROCHOL— Piazza du Plebiscito.
BRITISH LIBRERY AND READING ROOMS — Riviera di Chiaja N.º 267.
DURA J. — Strada de Chiaja N.º 10.
DUFRÉSNE E. — Medina N.º 61.

## Protestant Churches

FRENCH-GERMAN CHURCH — Via Carlo Poerio.

SCOTCH church — Strada Santa Maria a Cappella near Piazza dei Martiri.

ENGLISH CHURCH — Strada S. Pasquale a Chiaja.

SYNAGOQUE — Vico Cappella Vecchia a Chiaja.

---

Strangers, desirous of prolonging their stay at Naples, and wishing at the same time to avoid hotel expenses, will find here, as in all large towns, a number of well furnished appartments whose prices vary according to the situation. They are especially to be found in the streets of Chiatamone, Santa Lucia, Riviera di Chiaja, Giovanni Bausan, Mandella Gaetana, Santa Teresa a Chiaja and Mergellina.

In this case also we come to to the traveller's assistance, and give another series of addresses for all that a longer stay might necessitate.

## Master of languages

Emanuele Rocco  
Francesco Santini  } Italian language  
Professor Guarini  

M.r Decor  
M.r V. Leitnitz  } French language  

Miss Howard  
M.r Christie  } English language  

M.r Kaden  
M.r Kramer  } German language  
M.r Roeber  

*Nota.* — For addresses enquire at the music editors.

## Music Masters

| | |
|---|---|
| A. Quercia | Lanzilli Francesco |
| B. Carelli | S. Caracciolo |
| L. Andreatini | G. Scalera |
| C. Conti | F. Troîsi |
| V. Starace | S. Simonetti |
| C. Palumbo | C. De Crescenzo |
| D. Scafati | P. Serrao |
| F. Lanza | F. Coletti |
| P. Clemente | G. Grassi |
| M. Caputo | V. Galassi |
| B. Cesi | G. Pagano |
| G. Furno | E. Wenzel |
| G. Nacciarone | S. Gavaudan |
| S. Denza | E. Erra. |
| G. Tofano | F. Taglioni |
| E. Viceconte | G. Pagano |

*Note.* — For addresses enquire at the music editors.

## Hire of pianofortes and pianoforte makers.

Scognamiglio —Strada Carlo Poerio N.º 76.
Mach — Piazza dei Martiri Palazzo Calabritto.
Helzel — Strada de Chiaja N.º 138.
Sievers — Strada di Chiaia, Palazzo Francavilla.
Schmid — Strada Nardones N.º 51.
Heppler — Strada Nardones N.º 95.
P. Clausetti — Strada S. Carlo N.º 18.
**Music publishers** — Tito di Gio. Ricordi, Strada S. Carlo N.º 18—Girard, Str. Toledo, N.º 178 — Cottrau, Piazza del Municipio.
**School for young ladies** — Mad. Salis, Vico Calascione N.º .... Klein, Corso Vittorio Emanuole — palazzo Lucchesi.
Ducros — Vico Monteroduni N.º 8.
Doulet — Strada Bisignano N.º 48.
Caputo — Cappella vecchia.
Chiulli — Strada Cedronio N.º 27.
**School for young gentlemen** — Liebler — Monte di Dio N.º 74.
German school — Strada Egiziaca a Pizzofalcone N.º 60.
Scoppa — same Strada N.º 75.
César M. Nahmias—Riviera di Chiaja N.º 61.

However interesting a town might be, a traveller could not entirely occupy himself with antiquities and fine arts, and some change occasionally is needful. To this end, we give the notice of our principal theatres and of the clubs to which strangers may belong.

**Theatre of San Carlo**—by the side of the Royal palace. Grand opera and ballet.

**Theatre of the Fondo**—Strada del Molo—Dramas, prose tragedy and comedy.

**Teatro dei Fiorentini** — In the street of the same name. Same kind as the Fondo.

**National theatre**—Vico lungo Teatro Nuovo — Comedies and operettas.

**Teatro la Fenice** — Piazza del Municipio.

**Teatro San Carlino** — Operettas in the neapolitan patois.

---

**National Club** — Largo Vittoria N.° 5.

Honorary president H. R. H. the Prince of Piedmont.

Extract from the rules — Strangers even if they do not live at Naples can join this club as temporary members for the space of six months, on paying the sum of 150 francs for their right of entry. They may even be received for one month, on a written request signed by two permanent members of the club; and approved by a member of the committee. In this case the entrance fee is only 25 francs. Any one wishing to become a member of the club must be introduced by two permanent members.

**Casino dell'Unione**—In the same building as the San Carlo theatre — Through the introduction of the Board of administration, strangers of distinction, and their respective families, temporarily at Naples, may be invited to the reunions at the club. Strangers also, though passing several months at Naples, do not live there habitually, may be invited to join the club for eight days, either on the request of an established member or through the introduction of one of the members of the Board of direction. Wishing to join after the eight days they must ask to be received either as temporary members, as original or as ordinary members.

**Cercle de l'Academie**—Piazza San Ferdinando by the side of the Café d'Europe —

Extract from rules :

3rd Art. Strangers having no fixed residence

in Naples, and not wishing to belong to the Cercle as ordinary or original members may be enrolled simply as temporary members.

12th Art. Temporary members are taxed with a monthly payement of 17 francs payable in advance.

14th Art. To be received as a temporary member, the request must be signed and recommended by two original members and the admission will take place according to the same rules established for other members.

16th Art. Travellers may be invited to join the club gratuitously, for eight days, on the request of two original members, approved by one of the members of the deputation.

The eight days having elapsed, the entrance to the Cercle will be allowed them for one month on the payment of the sum of 17 francs

---

As Naples in spite of the salubrity of its climate, is not privileged to prevent any indisposition or accident that might happpen to distress the travaller, we add the following addresses.

**English Doctors**— D.r Wyatt—Strada Santa Catarina a Chiaja, palazzo Calabritto —

D.' Sammot — Strada S. Caterina a Chiaja palazzo Calabritto.

**German Doctors** = D.' Schrön — Strada Egiziaca a Pizzofalcone N.° 87 — D.' Obenaus — Via Gennaro Serra N.° 30.

**Homeopatic Doctors**—D.' Rubini —Strada Bisignano N. 45 — D.' Pelillo, Monte di Dio N.° 49 — D.' Longo, Strada Cavallerizza a Chiaja N.° 18.

**Italian Doctors** — D.' Ramaglia, Strada Santa Margherita a Fonseca.

D.' Lauro — Strada del Salvatore N.° 6.

D.' De Martino Antonio — Strada s. Potito, palazzo Ciccone.

D.' Semmola — Strada Trinità Maggiore N.° 6.

D.' Tommasi — Strada Tarsia N.° 6.

D.' Buonomo — Vicoletto S. Domenico Maggiore N.° 7.

D.' Cantani Arnaldo — Strada Tarsia, palazzo Tarsia.

D.' Caldarelli Antonio — Strada Pisanelli N.° 23.

D.' Lopiccoli — Vico delle Campane a Toledo N.° 3.

D.' Villanova — Strada Acqua Fresca di s. Paolo N.° 7.

D.ʳ Valerio Pasquale (*Maladies des oreilles*) — Strada Orticelli N.º 9.

**Surgeons**—D.ʳ Palasciano—Strada S. Carlo N.º 45.

D.ʳ Olivieri — Largo dei Bianchi allo Spirito Santo.

D.ʳ Amabile Luigi — Vico Rosario a Piazza Cavour palazzo Falanga.

**Accoucheurs** — D.ʳ Capuano — Strada Pignatelli N.º 12.

D.ʳ Tarsitani — Porta-Alba N.º 30.

D.ʳ Morisani — Vico Carrozzieri a Montoliveto N º 13.

**Oculists** — D.ʳ Novi Salvatore — Rue Alabardieri N.º 49 palazzo Filangieri.

D.ʳ Castorani — Strada Santa Lucia N.º 92.

**Dentists** — G. Gavaliere strada di Chiaia N.º 190.

J. Giové — Strada della Pace N.º 27.

# SECOND PART

A few hours stroll.

The brightest and finest quarters of Naples are those of St. Ferdinando, and the Chiaja situated to the west. The best streets are the Riviera di Chiaja, the Chiatamone, Santa Lucia, Toledo (now called Via Roma) the Corso Vittorio Emanuele, Foria and of the new streets, that of the Duomo which is not yet completed.

The public garden, or Villa Nazionale, is a beautiful walk bordering the sea in its graceful bend towards Mergellina. As horizon it has Vesuvius, the mountains of Castellamare and Sorrento, the island of Capri and the hill of Pausilippo. From May to the end of October the Villa is lit by gas the whole night, and concerts and amusements, which last up to 11 o'clock in the evenings, attract a numerous and select society. A band plays also all the afternoons of the other months.

Although Naples as regards squares, and places, has nothing of particular attraction we should not the less point out those considered the most remarkable and we place them in the following order.

1st Piazza del Plebiscito bordered by the Royal palace, the Basilica of St. Francisco di Paola, the palace of the Prefecture and that of the military Command. It is adorned with fine equestrian statues representing Charles 3rd and Ferdinand 4th of the Bourbons. The two horses and the statue of Charles are by Canova.

2nd Largo del Municipio, near the theatre of San Carlo, recently changed into a garden with fountains.

3d The new square before the railway station adorned with a fountain and group in marble by A. Buccini.

4th Piazza Cavour near the Museum also changed into a garden.

5th The piazza del Foro Carolino now Piazza Dante having in the middle the statue of the poet. The semi-circular building which terminates this square was constructed after a design of Vanvitelli.

6th Piazza dei Martiri a few steps from the

Riviera di Chiaja, in the centre of which is a monument erected by the town to the memory of the neapolitan citizens who died in the cause of liberty. This monument, made after a design of the Chevalier Henry Alvino, represents Victory crowning the revolutions of 1799, 1820, 1848 and 1860, simbolised by the lions at the base. The bronze statue was designed and cast by the Chevalier E. Caggiani.

Among the most remarkable fountains are those of Santa Lucia, the work of Merliani, that of Sebeto (via del Gigante) attributed to Fansaga; the Medina fountain in the street of the same name, commenced by D'Auria (1593) finished and embellished by the same Fansaga; that lately restored and placed in the via Piliero, the work of Bernini; finally the fountain of Montoliveto near the post office; the bronze statue on it representing Charles 2nd of Spain.

We must not however engage ourselves in the labyrinth of the streets, or we shall be compelled to halt at every step. Since also many travellers who come to Naples have only a a very little time at their disposal, let us pass at once to the more indispensable excursions and defer to the 3ᵈ part all of secondary interest, for those who are able to prolong their stay at Naples.

**The National Museum**, at the end of Toledo, is open every day, from 9 in the morning to 3 in the evening. The entrance is free Thursdays and Sundays ; other days 1 franc a head. This building, begun in 1587 by the viceroy the Duke of Ossuna, was completed by his successor, after the plans of J. Fontana. Intended, at first to serve as stables it became in turns University, and Barracks, seat of justice, university again, and in 1790 it was finally destined to hold artistic collections.

Its greatest importance accrues to it from the rich collections from Pompei, Cuma, Herculaneum and those vhich the king of Naples removed from his Farnese palace at Roma.

In giving a description of them we shall not follow the catalogne exactly, for that would draw us beyond the limits of this work, but we shall merely mention in each collection those objects vhich the visitor should especially notice. This choice made with as much exactitude as intelligence, allows us to state that a visit to the Museum following our directions, without fatiguing the traveller will have shown him all that is of the most important historical bearing in works of art. (1)

*Ground floor 1ˢᵗ door to the right entering under the peristyle.*

**Frescoes and Mosaics from Pompei and Herculaneum.**

This collection is composed of 72 groups marked in Roman characters. Let us pass the first gallery without stopping and enter on the right to see the numbers:

XIX. THE THREE PARTS OF THE ANCIENT WORLD symbolised by three women. P.

XXIX. PERSEUS DELIVERING ANDROMEDA FROM A SEA MONSTER P.

XXX. HERCULES DRUNK, SURROUDED BY LITTLE CUPIDS; NESSUS, DEJANIRA, HERCULES AND HIS SON HYTUS P.

XXXI. TELEPHUS FED BY THE DOE. The woman seated and crowned, the lion and the eagle symbols of Tegeus, a town of Peloponnesus. The other figures represent Hercules the god Pan and the goddess Fortune P.

---

(1) The place from which each object was taken is indicated by the initials P. Pompei, H. Herculaneum, F. Farnese, C. Cumae.

XXXVII. Theseus, after having slain the Minotaur P.

XXXVIII. The charge of Eneas, Anchises and Ascanius with dogs heads. P.

XXXIX. Carrying off Briseis from the tent of Achilles to take her to Agamennon. P.

XL. The sacrifice of Iphigenia P. A fine painting in which the father of the victim wrapped in a mantle, is hiding his face P.

XLI and XLIV. Twelve paintings representing rope dancers.

LI and LII. Cupid leading Bacchus and the sleeping Arianne P.

LIII. Thirteen dancers painted with infinite taste and grace P.

LIX. Three Greek paintings found at Poestum in a soldier's tomb. They represent warriors to whom women offer a cup.

LVIII. Italic paintings representing a funeral procession.

LXXII. Five monocromates among which we notice the three following. Latona, Niobbe and other women playing at dice, by Alexander of Athens (*read the inscription*). Another, depicting a tragic scene, and the third shewing Theseus delivering Hypodamia from the hands of a Centaur. H.

Before leaving this gallery the compartiment at the end should be visited where are seen.

**Mosaics.**

N. I. A Wrestler H.

N. III. Dog chained with the inscription Cave Canem P.

N. IV. Fish et Crustacae of surprising reality P.

N. V. Bacchic garland, festooned with leaves, fruits and flowers with two tragic masks. Above, another mosaic representing Bacchus on a Panther. P.

N. VII. A Director of a theatre (Choragus) distributing masks and dresses to his troupe. At the back of the picture are seen the columns of the theatre and by a seat on which a mask is thrown stands a flute player. It is one of the finest mosaics, and we call the particular attention of the connaisseur to it. It comes from the homeric house at Pompei. In this same group remark two other paintings, representing comic scenes The name of the author is read there (*Dioscourides of Samos*).

After seeing the mosaics, you return to the

first gallery of frescoes from which, by the door to the right, pass to the:

**Epigraphic collection** compresing 101 greek inscriptions; 58 inscriptions in ancient italic dialects; 1835 Latin; 184 Christian and 62 apochryphal inscriptions (or at least what one has every reason to believe such). All these inscriptions are classed in geographical order, according to the countries and towns, and those belonging to the same town are subdivided into three categories, sacred inscriptions, public or honourific and sepulchral.

*The first class*, comprising the Greek inscriptions, contains amongst others the celebrated bronze tables found at Herculaneum (numbers 81 and 82). The largest of these inscriptions has, on the back, the latter part of the municipal law called LEX JULIA. There is besides a *board* from Locri N.º 84 with an archaical inscription, and two marble columns N.º 1 and 2 with similar inscriptions belonging to the TRIOPIUM OF HERODE ATTICUS in the Appian way.

*The 2nd class* contains some Etruscan inscriptions of a secondary interest but there is the TABLE OF DE CRECCHIO in SABELLIC dialect, (N. 124), the BRONZE OF VELLETRI of great importance for the study of the volsque dialect, and finally the most beautiful collection of osque inscriptions amongst which is a fragment in two languages (osque and Latin) of a Roman law known by the name of TABLE BANTINA.

*The 3rd class*, richer than the others, comprises the Etruscan inscriptions, those of Latium, Ombria, Picene, Marsi, Samnium, Campania, Pouilles, Lucania, the Calabrias, Brutii, the public way, and many others of doubtful origin. Among the inscriptions of Rome the most important are the fragments of a bronze table (N.º 78) having in one of its sides the law REPETUNDARUM and in the other an agrarian law. After these are two other tables also of bronze ( Nᵐ 79 and 80 ) containing partly two laws dated the middle of the 7th century of Rome; then seventeen fragments of the ACTS ARVALICS ( N.º 57 and 73 ) and the base dedicated by the tribune SUCCUSANA to the rest of the family of Vespasian. Amongst the inscriptions found at Capua are seen many arcaiques of great importance.

The richest collection is that of sepulchral stones found at Pozzuoli and the other of inscriptions relating to soldiers and sailors of the fleet of Miseno. Under the head of graphic forms, the marbles of Herculanum and Pompei occupy the first place. Finally, in the class of christian inscriptions, we signalise 11 sepulchral stones of the consulary epoch.

From this room pass by the right into the gallery of the Bull and Hercules Farnese.

**Hercules Farnese.** This chef d'oeuvre of Grecian sculpture, by the Athenian Glycon, was found at Rome in the thermae of Caracalla where it had been taken from Athens by order of this emperor.

The right hand and toes are modern.

The statue represents Hercules resting, holding in his hand the three apples of the Hesperides.

Before the window is a calendar in marble known by the name of:

Farnese Calendar ( N.° 74 ) also found at Rome, divided into three parts, astronomical, rustic, and religious. The 1$^{st}$ marks the months, days and nights with their length, and the signs of the Zodiac. The 2$^{nd}$ shows agriculturers, the labours of each month, and the 3$^{rd}$ marks the religious feasts, and the devinities who preside over the months.

Near the stair-case in the centre of the room the numbers 1058 and 1059 show the: PUBLIC MEASURES for wheat, they are in marble with Latin inscriptions.

In this same gallery are two tables in bronze, that to the left contains inscriptions, among which we notice those of the years 1149 and 1168, explaining the leaves given to Roman soldiers, called *honestae missiones*. Stabia.

**The Farnese Bull.** This magnificent group formed of one single block of marble, found in the thermae of Caracalla was taken, according to Plinius, from Rhodes to Rome in the reign of Augustus, and it is thought to represent AMPHION and ZETHUS avenging the outrages of Dirce to their mother. They are exciting a bull to whose horns the victim is fastened by her hair. This group is attributed to two Grecian sculptors, APOLLONIUS and THARISCUS. Judging from the reliefs at the base, and from all the accessories, the scene took place on mount Citeron to which place Dirce had gone to celebrate bacchanals.

The wooden staircase in this gallery leads us to the EYPTIAN COLLECTION and to that of the CRISTIAN INSCRIPTIONS—Having nothing to signalise in the 1st room we pass straight to the 2nd where we notice:

N. 416 a small marble statue depicting the Goddess Isis, a cithern in her right hand, and the key of the Nile in the left. P. The inscription found at the foot of this statue informs us it was placed in the temple of Isis by order of the Decurions.

N. 68. Jupiter Serapis seated on the throne found in the famous temple of that name at Pozzuoli.

Against the wall are four lids of mummy cases in Sycamore wood, and at each side of the door leading to the next room are:

N. 942 and 944 two Ibis, sacred birds in Egypt P.

The last room opposite the entrance contains four Mummies from Thebes, and an embalmed Crocodile which was found wrapped up like a mummy. On the right side fixed to the wall is an:

Isiac table in calcareous stone. On the top are seen everal engraved figures amongst which:

Osiris with the head of a sparrow hawk.

**Collection of marbles.** To get to this collection we must entirely retrace our steps and in coming out under the peristyle turn towards the door opposite. 1st gallery:

N. 1. PTOLEMY SOTERUS. Roman sculpture H.

N. 4. GLADIATOR wounded in the thigh.

N. 26. ANOTHER GLADIATOR.

N. 45 (left side) AMAZON laid on her back, having a wound in the breast and both eyes half shut. F. At the end:

Large EQUESTRIAN STATUE of NONIO BALBO, son, found at Herculaneum 1839.

Near this statue, before the panel painted red, are two busts, that on the right represents Pompeus, the great, that on the left JULIUS BRUTUS. They were found at Pompei January 6th 1869.

N. 1736. A NEREID found at Pausilippo.

In the same gallery, to the right of the large equestrian statue, observe:

98. Venus and CUPID. Grecian sculpture found in the amphitheatre of Capua.

N. 78. STATUE OF JUNO, of great beauty. F.

N. 102. MINERVA, fighting against the Titans. H. At the end:

Equestrian statue of NONIO BALBO father.

On the opposite side, at the other end of this same corridor, is seen in a niche:

Colossal statue of Antinous with the attributes of Bacchus.

The door on the right leads to the collection of:

**Coloured marbles** 1st *room:* in the centre.

Apollo Citharede, in porphyr, one single piece, excepting the head, hands, and feet, which are of white Luni marble. In his left hand he holds a lyre, in his right a bow F.

N. 411. Statuette of Diana with a quiver on her back.

N. 215 Another statue of Diana in oriental alabaster. The extremities are bronze, the base porphyr F.

N. 232. Statue of Meleager in rossa antiqua P. The following room, in the centre.

N. 236. Large marble vase, with bas reliefs, by the Athenian Solpion, found at Formia near Gaeta.

By the side of this beautiful vase is the celebrated statue of:

Venus Gallypige in parian marble, a work of surpassing beauty, and of a most marvellous expression. It occupies one of the first places amongst the Greco-roman sculpture, and was found it seems in the celebrated golden house of Nero. F.

In this same room;

STATUE OF PSYCHE, fragments found in the amphitheatre Campano. Said to be the work of Praxitcles.

N. 336. BUST OF LYSIAS. The name engraved on the chest.

N. 580. BUST OF ZENON with the name in greek ZHENON.

HALL OF ADONIS; in the centre:

N. 267. STATUE OF ADONIS found in the amphitheatre Campano.

*In the next room.* A colossal statue of Hope or FLORA found, 1540, in the thermae of Caracalla. The head, one foot and part of the legs have been restored.

N. 138. MINERVA F. and opposite her:

JUNO F. both of great beauty.

ARISTIDES standing in the attitude of haranguing. H.

N. 131. ANTINOUS F.

In the centre:

LARGE MOSAIC found at Pompei in the house of the Faun, representing the battle of Issus, between Alexander and Darius. Twenty six figures are seen, a chariot and fifteen horses. It was injured by the catastrophe that destroyed Pompei.

Without stopping, let us cross the next room and pass to that of the:

**Marble bas-reliefs.**

N. 452. Sarcophagus with 18 figures F.

3rd *compartiment* BACCHUS SEATED with a panther at his feet. H.

N. 408. Other bas reliefs. ORPHEUS leading Eurydice from Hell with Mercury. Their names can be read there.

N. 358. *Caryatides*. At the foot of a tree is a woman seated and at either side two other women in Doric costume with a measure on their heads. The inscription is modern. *Pozzuoli*.

N. 320. BANQUET OF ICARIUS. Grecian bas reliefs in very good condition and of perfect execution. The figure of Bacchus, followed by Bacchantes and Fauns about to be seated at the banquet of Icarius. The god is here represented in his Indian character. Above is another bas-relief dipicting a bacchic procession H.

In the angle on the right in leaving:

N. 366. TIBERIUS ON HORSEBACK with a woman holding a torch and approaching the statue of Priapus. The horse is led by a slave. *Capri*.

N. 354. COMIC SCENE of a slave endeavouring to prevent his master striking one of his comrades. This latter trying to elude the blows meets another slave armed with a strap ready to execute his master's orders.

Above the sarcophagus:

N. 360. The TRIUMPHE OF SILENUS drunk on an ass supported on either side by two little Fauns whilst a Satyr holds up the ass which is stumbling. P.

N. 421. BACCHANAL composed of seven figures and a tigress. F.

N. 186. HELEN, VENUS, CUPID, PARIS and PITUS H.

In the same room in the centre is a pedestal erected to TIBERIUS by fourteen towns of Asia minor destroyed by an earthquake and rebuilt by order of this emperor. Each town is here symbolized by a woman at whose feet the name is engraved. (Read the inscription) *Pozzuoli.*

After visiting this room retracing our steps we regain the gallery or corridor of marbles where we saw the colossal statue of Antinous and through the door to the right we pass to the:

**Collection of bronze statues.—1st** *room.*

COLOSSAL HORSE'S HEAD in bronze which is supposed to have belonged to a large horse which stood under the portico of the temple of Neptune at Naples.

3.rd *room*, right side. near the window:
STATUE OF NERO. H.
STATUE OF LIVIA, wife of Augustus. H.

N. 52. HALF BUST OF ARCHYTAS, the head adorned with a band of woven woolly feathers of Tarant, which was given to illustrious men. H.

THREE ACTRESSES OR DANCERS with glass-eyes H.

N. 29. HALF BUST OF PTOLEMY SOTERNS. H.

N. 61. Half bust of PTOLEMY APION.

N. 39. HALF BUST OF PTOLEMY ALEXANDER. H.

N. 31. BUST OF PTOLEMY PHILADEPHUS. H.

N. 25. HALF BUST OF BERENICE, one of the finest portraits existing in the Museum found in 1756. The lips and eyes were incrusted with silver. H.

N. 14. PTOLEMY PHILOMETORE, father of Berenice. H. *Opposite:*

Other actresses from the theatre at Herculaneum. In the centre of this room notice:

YOUNG SLEEPING FAUN. A SITTING MER-

CURY. HALF BUST OF SENECA, the finest of all found of him. HALF BUST OF ZEUSIPPO. The TWO DISCOBULI. A DRUNKEN FAUN leaning on a half-empty skin. All these busts and statues come from Herculaneum. Statue of APOLLO. P. Another APOLLO in the act of discharging an arrow. P.

In the last room; on a column:

N. 46. BUST OF SCIPIO AFRICANUS with two wounds on the head. H.

N. 36. BUST OF HERMES supposed to be of Augustus. H. The name of the sculptor can be read, Apollonio.

In the same room:

**Collection of armour and arms** classed in the following order:

1st *cabinet*: GRECIAN ARMS AND ARMOUR found at POESTUM, RUVO and CANOSA.

2nd *cabinet*: ROMAM AND ITALIC ARMS from Pompei, Pozzuoli, Herculaneum and Pietrabbondante.

3d *cabinet*: ARMS FOR GLADIATORS, coming from Herculaneum and Pompei.

N. 283. A HELMET RICHLY DECORATED with reliefs referring to the Trojan war.

Under the window. 2nd *compartment*:

GLANDS MISSILI, supposed to have belonged to Cesar's troops who used them against the armes of Azio Varo.

3ᵈ *compartment*:

N. 93. Remmants of a bone cuirass. P.

Our visit to the ground floor is nearly done. No more remains but to see the last portico on the left of the large staircase where one should stop to admire :

The beautiful STATUE OF AGRIPPINA the grandmother of Nero, taken from the Farnese collection.

The BUST OF ANTONINUS AND FAUSTINA on the sides of the alcove. At the end, under a globe :

A STORK holding a lizard in its beak.

Going up the staircase, the entresol on the right contains the :

**Collection of objects of the 15ᵗʰ century,** and *Glasses and terra-cotta from Pompei.*

N. 430. LARGE BRONZE BAPTISTERY in the centre of the first room of octagon shape, having on each side the miracles of Jesus in bas reliefs. This beautiful monument is attributed to the school of Michaelangelo. it was taken from the Certosa of S.ᵗᵃ Maria degli Angeli at Rome to the Convent of S.ᵗ Lorenzo della Padula, in the province of Salerno.

N. 29. Fastened to the wall another MARBLE BAS-RELIEF REPRESENTING THE PASSION OF OUR LORD in the style of the German renaissance. It was placed in the Church of S.' Giovanni a Carbonara.

In the centre of the 2$^{nd}$ room on a marble table:

VERMILION BOX; it is shaped like a rectangular temple, and at the angles are the allegorical figures of Venus, Bacchus, Minerva and Mars leaning against quadrupeds, in their turn supported by sphinxes. Eight Caryatides adorn its angles, and two others dividing into two the larger facings of the casket, form altogether six little panels in which are raised as many medallions in rock crystal with engravings representing:

1$^{st}$ A COMBAT BETWEEN GREEKS AND AMAZONS.

2$^{nd}$ COMBAT OF CENTAURS.

3$^{d}$ A NAVAL COMBAT.

4$^{th}$ HUNTING THE WILD BOAR CALEDONIO.

5$^{th}$ A BACCHANAL.

6$^{th}$ THE GAMES OF THE CIRCUS.

The roof forming the lid of the box represents in bas reliefs, the three great epochs in the life of Hercules whose statue surmounts the monument. In the interior to the right of the box is the apotheosis of Hercules. At the bottom Alexander the Great to whom a slave presents a box containing the works of Homer the only thing he kept out of the booty taken from the Persians. Finally above the lid is another bas relief alluding to the instability of the things of this world.

This admirable work came from the Farnese family and was executed at the beginning of the 16$^{th}$ century by Giovanni de Bernardo of Castel Bolognese.

**Glasses**—3$^{rk}$ *room*, near the window place.

BLUE VASE in shape of an amphora resting on a modern silver pedestal. This beautiful work rests on a plan decorated with animals in white glass. P.

N. 2776. BEAUTIFUL GLASS dish of many colours. *Ruvo.*

BLUE GLASS CUP ornamented in the middle with a mask of Silenus. The handle is finished with a sheep's head in white enamelled glass.P.

**Terra cotta** — 5$^{th}$ *room*.

TWO STATUES OF JUPITER AND JUNO. P.

On leaving this collection we go to the first floor on the left hand side, where first of all we must visit the collection of:

**Impressions** — In this room are collected several marble busts and some cartoons of Raphael and Michaelangelo. We begin with:

Bust of Dante, life size and which is thought to have been taken from the features of the great poet.

N. 1. Marble bust of Paul 3$^{rd}$ Farnese.

N. 7. Gian Gaston de Medicis, marble.

N. 32. Fernando de Medicis, marble.

**Cartoons of Raphael and Michael-Angelo.**

N. 3. The Holy Family.

N. 4. Cupid and Venus.

N. 5. Moses before the burning bush done for one of the halls in the Vatican.

N. 2. Sacrifice with several figures, author unknown.

**Collection of cuttings** in the large cabinet, very rich and rare, whose number exceeds 1900. It is called the Firmiana collection from the name of its first owner of whom the Bourbons bought it. King Victor Emmanuel presented it to the Museum.

In the same cabinet are:

Three silver planks which belong to the Farnese family. On one of these planks, representing a bacchanal, is engraved the name of Annibal Caracci. Another, square shaped, represents a group, and the third a *descent from the cross* by the same Caracci, dedicated to Cardinal Salvati in 1598 (See the words engraved in one of the corners). At the back are the initials A. C. I. I. (Annibal Caracci invented and engraved).

In leaving this gallery you enter the picture galleries on the left.

**Hall of Polydorus**—*Roman school* containing 57 canvasses—*Parmense school* containing 39 canvasses.

**Hall of Cesare da Sesti**—*Lombards and Parmensi* 39 canvasses — *Venetian school* 59 pictures. — From this room you pass to the:

**Hall of Correggio** containing 16 pictures:

N. 1. JESUS DISPUTING WITH THE DOCTORS, by Salvator Rosa.

N. 2. THE HOLY FAMILY. Painting on slate by Sebastiano Luciani called del Piombo.

N. 3. VIRGIN under the name of THE ZINGARELLA OR MADONNA DEL CONIGLIO. Painting on wood by Antonio Allegri called Correggio.

N. 4. PORTRAIT OF AN UNKNOWN. Van Dyck.

N. 5. DANAE AND CUPID smiling at the transformation of Jupiter, by Titien Vecellio.

N. 6. JESUS SLEEPING, by Correggio (on wood).

N. 7. By the same. THE MYSTIC MARRIAGE OF S.' CATHERINE (on wood).

N. 8. PORTRAIT OF PAUL 3ᵈ, by Titian.

N. 9. DESSENT FROM THE CROSS (on wood) by Correggio.

N. 10. THE HOLY VIRGIN leaning her head on the infant Jesus, by Correggio (tempera).

N. 11. PORTRAIT OF PHILIP 2ⁿᵈ OF SPAIN, by Titian.

N. 12. S.' SEBASTIAN, by Ribera called Spagnoletto.

N. 13. S.' JEROME alarmed at the sound of the trumpet at the last judgment. Ribera.

N. 14. By the same. S.' JEROME in meditation.

N. 15. THE MAGDALEN repenting, by Guercino.

N. 16. HEAD OF A MONK, by Rubens (on wood).

**Hall of Raphael:**

N. 17. HOLY FAMILY, OR THE MADONNA DEL GATTO, by Giulio Romano (on wood).

N. 18. PORTRAIT OF THE CHEVALIER TIDALDEO, by Raphael (on wood).

N. 19. PORTRAIT OF AN UNKNOWN, by J. Bellini (on wood).

N. 20. HOLY FAMILY, by Raphael (on wood).

N. 21. LEO 10ᵗʰ AND THE CARDINALS DE ROSSI AND DE MEDICIS, by Raphael (on wood).

N. 22. PORTRAIT OF CARDINAL PASSERINI by Raphael (on wood).

N. 23. THE VIRGIN AND INFANT JESUS by Bernardino Luini (on wood).

N. 24. PORTRAIT OF CLEMENT 7ᵗʰ by Andrea Vannucchi called Andrea del Sarto (on wood).

N. 25. THE ADORATION OF THE MAGI, by Luca Damnez called Luca d' Olanda (on wood).

N. 26. CHRIST ON THE CROSS, by Giovanni Emmeling (on wood).

N. 27. THE PARABLE OF THE BLIND MEN, by Breuguel (tempera).

N. 28. NATIVITY OF JESUS, by Albert Durer (on wood).

N. 29. VIRGIN AND INFANT JESUS, by Perugino (on wood).

N. 30. PORTRAIT OF AN UNKNOWN, by Scipio Pulzone called Scipio of Gaeta (on brass).

N. 31. S.ᵗ JEROME drawing the thorn from the lion's foot, by J. de Bruges (on wood).

N. 32. THE LAST JUDGMENT, by Marcello Venusti (on wood). Copy from the large picture, by Michael-Angelo, in the Sistine Chapel.

N. 33. TRANSFIGURATION OF JESUS, by Giovanni Bellini (on wood).

N. 34. HOLY FAMILY, by Giovanni Spagna.

N. 35. ROMAN LUCRETIA, by Francesco Mazzuoli called Parmigianino (on wood).

N. 36. THE VIRGIN AND SAINTS, by Santafede (on wood).

*Large room* of different schools containing 60 pictures. Then the *Hall of Venus* containing 38 pictures also of different schools.

From this room, in coming out on the great staircase, go through the middle door to the:

**Library** whose foundation is due to Paul 3$^d$ Farnese. It contains more than 200,000 volumes amongst which about 4000 are editions of the 15$^{th}$ century, and 400 manuscripts in Greek, Latin, Italian, Arabic, Chinese, Persian etc. Among the most ancient of these manuscripts are *two papyrus* in Latin, and among the *autographs* those of S.' Thomas, Gian Battista Vico, Tasso, Mazzocchi etc. This library is open to the public every day from 9 in the morning to 3 in the afternoon, and, for a slight recompense, blind people can be read to.

In leaving, first go down by the left, then up the staircase facing you, and, by the first door on the right, enter the:

**Room of stones, cameos** etc. In the window on the right is:

A PIECE OF CLOTH OF AMIANTE found in a tomb in 1835 in the Abruzzi, and FRAGMENTS OF IVORY STATUES. P.

1$^{st}$ *cabinet*: LOAVES found in an oven at Pompei.

2$^{nd}$ *cabinet*: FIGS, NUTS, LAMP WICKS, PRUNES, WHEAT etc.

6$^{th}$ *cabinet* 1$^{st}$ *compartment*:

N. 1, 2, 3, 4, A BRACELET, TWO EARRINGS, and A NECKLACE, found by the side of a skeleton in the house of Arrius Diomede. P.

2$^{nd}$ *compartment*: N. 422 BEAUTIFUL NECKLACE WITH MASKS (Venosa province of Basilicata).

TWO SMALL CYLINDRIC VASES in gold, containing two little glass flasks for perfumes, coming also from Venosa.

A NECKLACE OF GARNETS found near S.$^t$ Agatha of the Goths, province of Caserta.

3$^d$ *compartment*: TWO BRACELETS OF SPIRAL form of marvellous execution, and others.

7$^{th}$ *cabinet* 1$^{st}$ *compartment*: TWO PATRICIEN BULLAE P. and H.

**Objects in silver.** 8$^{th}$ *cabinet* 4$^{th}$ *compart.* N. 215, 218, 222, TRIPODS used at sacrifices.

*Last cabinet* 1st *compartment*: N. 14. THE MOST BEAUTIFUL VASE found at Herculaneum. It is in the form of a mortar decorated with bas reliefs depicting the history of Homer whose two chief works are personified by two beautiful figures seated on foliage. That on the right represents the Odyssey holding a rudder, and that on the left the Iliad as a warrior.

2nd *compartment*: BRONZE sun dial covered with silver leaf. H.

N. 59 *in the same compartment*: A ROUND MIRROR with an engraving on the back of the death of Cleopatra.

On a column near the balcony is:

The CELEBRATED FARNESE CUP in oriental sardonyx found at Rome in Adrian's Villa, unique for the size of the stone and the perfection of the work. It belongs to the Augustan epoch. The HEAD OF MEDUSA is seen, and on the other side, seven figures of men and a sphinx. The best admitted interpretation of the engraving is Ptolemy Philadelphus consacrating the feast of the harvest.

**Cameos** — 1st *table* 1st *compartment* to the left.

N. 5. NEPTUNE AND PALLAS (onyx) disputing which of their names should be given to Athens.

N. 16. Jupiter in quadrige (onyx).

N. 19. Head of Omphale (sardonyx).

N. 29. Omphale sleeping, bent on Hercule's club.

N. 44. The head of Augustus in sardonyx attributed to Dioscorides.

N. 48. Bacchus on the shoulders of a Faun (onyx).

N. 64. The punishment of Dirce, fragment in agate.

**Engraved stones** — Table divided in two compartments. *In the first*, on the left:

N. 219. Perseus, the name of the maker Dioscorides engraved on it.

N. 232. Diana as untress.

2.$^{nd}$ *compartment*:

N. 373. A woman's head in sardonyx.

N. 390. Sacrifice with several figures (cornelian).

N. 413. Bust of Pescennio (see the inscription) (cornelian).

6$^{th}$ *table. Only one compartment.*

N. 1755. Ring found at Herculaneum. King Charles 3$^{rd}$ wore it on his finger, and when he had to leave Naples, gave it to the Museum.

N. 478. ANOTHER RING IN FILAGREE with an emerald forming a box.

**Pornographic Collection** — This room which is paved with a Pompeian mosaic contains pagan monuments. On the wall are several frescoes, two standards with a Latin inscription and some mosaics. Notice particularly a marble sculpture representing :

A SATYR WITH A GOAT, takem from Pompei.
A BRONZE TRIPOD H.

*In the cabinet* are lamps, amulets and statuettes. Before leaving, observe two glass bottles containing oil, lately discovered at Pompei. The door on the right leads to the second collection of pictures.

**Room of the Caracci** — *Bolognese school* containing 75 pictures — *Tuscan school* containing 58 pictures — *Neapolitan school* 14$^{th}$ 15$^{th}$ and 16$^{th}$ century 36 pictures. — Another room, *ancient Byzantin and Tuscan* containing 59 pictures.

— *Neapolitan school* 13$^{th}$ and 14$^{th}$ centuries containing 14 pictures. — *The same school* 16$^{th}$ 17$^{th}$ and 18$^{th}$ centuries containing 96 pictures.

— *German, Flemish and Dutch schools* containing 43 pictures.

— *Flemish and Dutch schools* containing 98 pictures.

**Collection of small bronzes** — In the centre of the *first room* on a marble table

N. 473. CANDELABRE one of the finest found in the house of Diomed at Pompei.

IRON BAR FOR THE CONDEMNED, found in the soldier's barracks at Pompei. Four skeletons, were attached to it.

On an ancient table is:

ECONOMICAL STOVE made with an iron plank for holding fire, and a cylindric vase for water, the lid of the vase is ornamented with a head of Mercury.

In the *first cabinet on the right* is seen:

A SMALL CANDELABRE representing a little Cupid on a dolphin which is devouring a polypus. P.

N. 505. THREE BEAKED LAMP ornamented with masks and garlands. H.

N. 1325. CYLINDRIC LANTERN IN TALC LEAF. (House of Diomed at Pompei).

In the following cabinets we mention, as curiosities, *several kitchen utensils, pieces of furniture and dress, weights of different sizes in serpentine stone, porphyry and lead. Measures for liquids and corn. A*

*weight for liquids, compasses, linear measures, leads for levelling, several small scales, etc. etc.*

In one of the cabinets are:

NINE LARGE SCALES hooked to the wall, among which we notice the 4$^{th}$ on the right, of which the cup is of fine work and upheld by four little chains. The balance represents the bust of an Emperor armed with helmet and cuirass.

*Second room in the centre:*

N. 1389. Seat of honour, without back. H. On a mosaic table is:

N. 1. A BEAUTIFUL TRIPOD.

BACCHIC LECTISTERNES encrusted with silver and a red mastic. H.

In one of the cabinets are:

SURGICAL INSTRUMENTS.

A LITTLE PORTABLE KITCHEN in the form of a rampart with towers at the corners. In the spaces between the battlements are the spits for roasting. H.

N. 2900. A BELL. P.

*In the last cabinet*

TWO PAILS WITH HANDLES encrusted with silver. On one of the handles is seen the owner's name, *Cornelia Chelidone*. H.

KETTLE resembling those now used Russia for tea.

*Last room at the bottom:*

THREE BEDS lately found at Pompei encrusted in silver. They are placed in the same order in which they were found.

THREE CASES of fine work.

In retracing our steps, before leaving, we notice on the right the collection of:

**Italo-Greco Vases** — This collection contains about 4,000 vases of various sizes and colours, nearly all with figures or other images of religious bearing and used for domestic purposes. They were enclosed in tombs with other objects such as necklaces, arms, bracelets etc. All the rooms of this collection are paved with mosaics from Pompei, Herculaneum and Stabia.

Remark in the 2nd *room*:

MINIATURE MODELS of two tombs discovered at S.' Agatha of the Goths, and at Poestum.

N. 2718. LARGE VASE decorated with a fight between Greeks and Amazons, found at *Canosa*.

N. 2034. ORESTES TORMENTED BY THE FURIES. *Capua*.

N. 3231 (red) Marsyas condemned to be flaged. *Capoa.*

N. 1979. Dædalus placing the wings on Icarus. *Pouilles.*

N. 1183. Vase with bows. Very rare on account of the handles. *Cuma.*

N. 2716. Vase with grotesque heads and figures representing Archemorus dying and Hercules in the Hesperides. *Ruvo.*

N. 3253. Large historic vase of great price. Darius consulting his ministers on the war against the Greeks.

*Near the balcony:*

N. 200. Vase for perfumes, very rare, on account of the bas reliefs. Marsyas is here represented fastened to a pine and flaged alive for defying Apollo in music. This god, and the Muses, assist at the punishment. The executioner holds the skin of Marsyas. *Canosa.*

N. 2774. Vase with masks. Achilles in his chariot drawing the body of Hector round the walls of Troy. *Ruvo.*

N. 2360. Urn with three handles, found in a tomb at Nola. This superb vase represents the exploits of Eneas in the Trojan war. In the centre is Pyrrhus slaying Priam, the latter with his son Ajax on his knees about

64

to carry off Cassandra from the Palladium of Minerva. Finally, Eneas escaping with his father Anchises and his son Ascanius.

N. 2421. VASE WITH COMBAT. *Ruvo:*

N. 2419. ANOTHER VASE UNDER A SHADE WITH LID on which is figured THE NEONIA FEAST which the Greeks celebrated in the Autumn in the honour of Bacchus. *Nola.*

4$^{th}$ *room* on a pedestal:

N. 2024. BELL OF BARI, in Greek is read *Asteas designed.*

*Last room:*

LARGE VASE on which is represented Pluto in his palace with Proserpine. Above Minos, then Hercules with Cerberus, Orpheus conducting Euridice etc. At the foot the Stygian river. *Ruvo.*

Then a large number of glasses in fancy shapes.

**The Santagelo Collection** merits a visit from the importance of its vases and medals of ancient Italy.

**Cumana Collection**, on the middle floor on the right going down. A few minutes will suffice as there are only two objects worthy attention. *In the 2$^{nd}$ room,*

A WAX MASK found in a tomb enclosing

four headless skeletons; and on a pedestal near the window :

PRETTY LITTLE VASE of beautiful design, enamelled in black on which is depicted a combat between Greeks and Trojans.

As accessory to the Museum, we must here place the :

**Certosa of S.' Martino**, near the Castle of S.' Elmo. You drive there by the street Salvator Rosa, or go on donkeys by the Petrajo. These donkeys can be got at the Pjazza San Carlo alle Mortelle and the price at the most is 50 centimes.

— The Certosa was founded in the 14th century by Charles the son of Robert of Anjou, and the artistic wealth it contains entitles it to be classed among the first in Italy.

— Before entering the Church under the portico are seen FRESCOES OF MICCO SPADARO AND OF BELLISARIO in rather bad condition. Inside, the walls of the Church are encrusted with beautiful marbles of different colours, an admirable work executed by Cosimo Fansaga, who had them brought expressly from Carrara. To this artist are also attributed the twelve rosasses in Egyptian basalt placed in the interior of the pillars supporting the vaults of the chapels, as well as the pavement of the chancel equally encrusted in marble. For the paintings we name first the FRESCOES of the roof by Lanfranco, the pictures by Spagnoletto representing MOSES AND ELIAS, a NATIVITY by Guido Reni, a DESCENT FROM THE CROSS by Stanzioni, and at the side of the altar JESUS ADMINISTERING EUCHARIST TO THE APOSTLES also by Spagnoletto.

On the altar in the Tesoro Nuovo must be noticed the magnificent picture of PIETY, by the same Spagnoletto, and in the Sacristy, the BEAUTIFUL PAINTING BY THE CHEVALIER D'ARPINO. A fine work in MARQUETERIE in the same Sacristy, contains the Church ornaments.

— The roof of the Chapter is adorned with FRESCOES BY CORENZIO, and behind the church, the cloister serving formerly as cemetery for the monks, is a little master piece of doric architecture by Fansaga.

We should never be able to finish a detailed account of all that this convent and Church contain in paintings, sculpture and objects of art of all kinds. Neither can we mention a special Guide, for the only one we know of, published in 1854, by Raffaele Tufari, is now very rare.

A Museum of neapolitan history is being formed in this place by Commendatore Fiorelli director of the national Museum, which adds much to its interest. We can point out some of the most important objects already placed there. — COLLECTION OF THE MAJOLICHE DI CASTELLO — VENETIAN GLASS — CAPODIMONTE CHINA — SILK AND ARRAS of the ancient Neapolitan fabrics; all this belonging once to the Commendatore Bonghi, and known by the name of the BONGHI COLLECTION — The GALA CARRIAGE belonging to the Municipality of Naples, and the FLAGS that were presented to the church of S.' Lorenzo, for vows made during the plague in the year 1656. As historical curiosity is to be seen the HAT of Cardinal Ruffo a well known personage in the Neapolitan history — The CHAIR of the president of the house of parliament in the year 1848, manuscripts, newspapers etc. etc. The hours of admission are from 9 to 3 p. m. and in the summer till 5. However let us not omit to see from the end of the corridor one of the most beautiful panoramas imaginable.

Near the Certosa is the :

**Castle of S. Elmo** founded in 1342 by order of Robert the Wise, as the means of keeping the people in subjection and repressing all revolutionary movement in the town. Besieged at different periods, this castle has no longer any defensive importance since the invention of cannons (rayés).

---

### Excursion to Pompei.

Without doubt this is the most interesting excursion. The length of the journey by the railroad is only 45 minutes, the same driving two hours. The ordinary price of a carriage for four, going and returning, and stopping at the ruins, is from 15 to 20 francs. This is preferable if one wishes to visit at the same time the ruins of Herculaneum ; but if intending to make the ascent of Vesuvius it would be as well to do these two last the same day, and to make the journey to Pompei by rail.

To see Pompei well, there will be some hours walking, therefore a halt for refreshments is necessary. Lunch can be had at one of the Restaurants at the entrance to the town, but it would be better to take provisions from Naples and eat them in the midst of these interesting ruins. For procuring cold provisions refer to the addresses in the 4$^{th}$ part.

The entrance to Pompei is free only on Sundays. On other days 2 francs each person. By subscription ticket, 15 francs for ten entrances, subscribers have the right of leaving the excavations and returning after lunch paying nothing extra. For these subscriptions apply at the bureau of the Secretariat of the National Museum. Artists have the privilege of free entrance ; if strangers they must prove themselves to be artists by showing the Secretary a certificate from their Consul, or from the Director of the Institution of Fine Arts at Naples.

On entering Pompei each visitor receives a little card which allows him to visit the town in every direction, and to receive all information from one of the guides to whom is expressly forbidden to ask or receive any recompense.

The town of Pompei, almost entirely destroyed by an earthquake at the commencement of our Era, had not recovered from the havoc caused by this catastrophe when, in the year 79 it was buried, as well as Stabia, Retina and Herculaneum, under a shower of boiling water, volcanic cinders and lapilli ejected from Vesuvius. This last catastrophe lasted no less than three days.

If we may believe certain savants, the beautiful plain separating Pompei from Castellammare called Messigna, was a bay which was filled up by this vulcanic eruption. This opinion founded besides on the study and scientific analysis of the soil, has been confirmed by the discovery of several masts buried in the ground 40 feet deep in the same place now still called *La Marina*.

The barbarians having destroyed the finest monuments of Latium, Campania and Sybaris, the disaster which struck Pompei, saved it from the effects of their fury, and its unique merit is in having furnished, besides the preservation of its monuments and houses, a host of objects which reveal the private life of the Latin populations.

The most remarkable ruins of Pompei are the House of the Faun, the Basilica, the Temple of Jupiter, the Triumphal Arch, the Public Seat, the Temple of Fortuna, the STABIAN THERMAE, the CIVIL FORUM, the HOUSE OF THE TRAGIC POET, that of PANSA, the AMPHITHEATRE, the TEMPLE OF NEPTUNE, and the VILLA DIOMED.

From the mere mention of these buildings from which the most interesting debris have been taken to the Museum, the traveller will understand the importance of this excursion.

He can appreciate not only the good taste of the Pompeians in fine arts, but also their habits, and the curious double existence of public and private life to be remarked always amongst the ancients.

The pompeian houses generally had two stories, sometimes three, and were covered by a roof or by a terrace called *Pergula.* The public portion had always its vestibule, *Prothyrum*; a court, *Atrium*, in a corner of which a little temple, *Lararium*, and all around a portico, *Cavaedium*; then the chamber of audience, *Tablinum*; and on each side, *Alae*, two open waiting-rooms; from these and the *Tablinum* a corridor, *Fauces*, that leads to the women's apartements.

The private portion generally looking into a garden had the men's apartments, *Andronitis* and that of the women, *gynaeconitis*; the dining room, *Triclinium*, and next the, *Exedra* for winter dining room ; the kitchen and its accessories, *Culine*; the *Bibliotheca*; the *Pinacotheca*; the bath room, *Nymphaeum*; and another larger garden, *Xystus*, with porticos for amusements in the summer. The little rooms on the second floor, and sometimes others over these, *Coenacula*, served as depots for provisions, or if they were separate, they were let. The paintings and mosaics which decorated their rooms were descriptive of their usages.

The slaves, *Ostiarii*, had the charge of the entrances and lived in rooms adjoining those of their masters as to be always at their ordres.

We recommend the traveller to give a coup d'oeil to the best work which has been published on Pompei « Le case e monumenti di Pompei » by the brothers Nicolini. This book is rare but there is a copy in the library of the Museum at Naples.

The Commendatore Fiorelli superintendant of the Museum at Naples and of the excavations at Pompei has thought of introducing plaster into the cavities found in the ashes and sand. By this means he has obtained the shapes of the doors, windows, beds and furniture, and what is still more wonderful of some of the episodes of the tragedy of Pompei; such as the father dead by the side of his daughter, the pregnant woman and the slave which are seen in the museum at Portamarina at Pompei. The girl has a gold ring on her finger, the slave an iron one. The excavations continually advance and further labours in the course of time will expose completely the southern limits of the city.

In going to Pompei you see the towns of PORTICI and RESINA, pristine places of the LAGRIMA CHRISTI wine well known and justly appreciated by wine tasters and exported to all countries.

Then comes TORRE DEL GRECO, emporium of the commerce of coral and coral fishery; and next TORRE ANNUNZIATA where the government has a manufactory of arms, and where the entire population is occupied in making *maccaroni* and other edible pastes known as Italian pastes.

A little beyond Pompei is the small town of SCAFATI possessing a fabric of gun powder and a dyeing establishment of *Adrianople Red* of which great use is made in Africa, and which is extracted from maddler cultivated in the province of Salerno and in the fields of Castellammare.

---

**Herculaneum** much resembles Pompei. In the one as in the other the streets are paved and bordered with pavements. There is the same architecture, the same paintings, mosaics, and household utensils.

Many statues have been taken to the Museum and the finest are the two equestrian statues of Nonio Balbo and his son. The discovery of a large number of Papyrus made at Herculaneum has given it still greater importance. The remains of food, bread, eggs, fruits, vegetables etc. can be seen at the Museum.

The greater part of this town is still buried under the lava and scoria and the most interesting buildings discovered are those of the Theatre, the Basilica, and the two houses of Argus and Aristides.

---

**Pozzuoli — Baja — Cumae.**
In making this excursion we pass through

the Grotto of Pozzuoli or Pausilippo. In all probability the Cumeans wishing to shorten the road between their town and Naples, dug this passage whose level has since been lowered which is visible on entering. The village, on leaving the grotto, is called Fuori Grotta and beneath the vestibule of the little Church of S.' Vitale is the tomb of the philologist and poet Giacomo Leopardi. Stopping in the centre of the place we have on the right the Camaldoli, on the left the hill of Pausilippo and opposite us a plain extending to the sea. Then two roads the one leading to Pozzuoli the other to the lake of Agnano now dried up. We will not leave without visiting the basin of this lake, from which by a cross road, we can regain our first route. Archeologians do no agree on the etymology of the word *Agnano*. According to some it comes from the Latin *anguis* ( serpent ) as all that country is infested by these reptiles. According to others, it takes its origin from the name of a Roman family *Anniani*, who had a large property in this place.

Arriving at the basin of the lake we find at first the Thermae Angoulanae or Baths of S.ᵗ Germano so called because S.ᵗ Germano, archbishop of Capua, tried them for his health. A little further on the right is the LITTLE GROTTO, called DEL CANE, because a dog cannot live there without being asphyxiated. This phenomenon is soon explained: from the soil of this grotto carbonic acid is perpetually rising and does not come up above a certain level which is about a dog's height. It therefore follows that one of these animals compelled to breathe this gas is asphyxiated in a few seconds. It would be equally fatal for any animal of the same height, but as since the discovery of this grotto dogs have always been used to test its effect, it has been called after them. Instead of subjecting a dog to this cruel experiment one could satisfy oneself by trying it with a light, which on nearing the ground, is immediately extinguished. Further on the GROTTO called DELL'AMMONIACA presents the same phenomenon. A franc is generally given to the guardian.

Following the borders of the lake, in the same westerly direction, we come to a road leading to the hills LEUCOGEI or WHITE MOUNTAINS, at the foot of which is the thermo-mineral source OF THE PISCIARELLI, to which peasants have recourse for diseases of the skin. It seems these hills furnished the Campani with an edible earth, which they employed in the preparation of certain dishes instead of fecula.

From these same hills is extracted Trachyte decomposed by the action of hot sulphureous vapours, and used in making the alum of Naples of which the exportation constitutes an important branch of commerce. After this we may leave the lake and by the beautiful walk fronting us reach the high road of Pozzuoli.

Arrived on the sea shore, let us look a moment at the splendid panorama before us. On the East the Island of Nisida with its ancient port, on the West the Flegrean fields, on the South Pozzuoli, Cape Miseno, the Monte Nuovo, Baja, Avernus and the Elysian fields, a little further the island of Procida whose charming peasant women preserve intact their grecian costume and, at the end of the picture, the gigantic Epomeo (Isle of Ischia).

This place, called the Bagnoli, abounds in sources of thermo-mineral waters which is proved by the many establishments for baths to be seen on the way. Turning from thence to the right after going along the side of a mountain formed exclusively of volcanic rock (Mount Olibano) we come to POZZUOLI formerly the emporium of CUMAE and the CAMPANIA FELICE, and the stay of commerce between Europe and Asia. For a moment let us leave this town and first ascend the :

**Solfatara** — On arriving at Pozzuoli the traveller is beset by a crowd of guides. One of these men is quite sufficient to show the Solfatara and the antiquities near the town. The ordinary fee is about 1 fr. 50 centimes, but it is better to decide the price before starting. The Solfatara is a crater of a half extinct volcano, the ground of which is hollow and resounds when a stone is thrown upon it. For centuries the phenomenon of a slow and invariable combustion has been remarked in this crater, and in other places of the Flegrean regions.

Descending we find :

**The Amphitheatre**, larger than those of Pompei and Verona, but not so vast as those of Rome and Capua not holding above 35,000 persons. It was there S.' Januarius, and other martyrs, were shut up to be devoured by wild beasts. Some steps from the Amphitheatre are:

**The Theatre,** of circular shape, the ruins of ancient thermae called the TEMPLE OF DIANA and OF NEPTUNE, the VILLA OF CICERO, and the TEMPLE OF SERAPIS discovered in 1750.

This last temple, no doubt constructed on a ground constantly dry, sank later 5 metres below the level of the sea, and retook afterwards its primitive position. As the level of the Mediterranean has not changed, this phenomenon cannot otherwise be explained than by the oscillations of the ground and the general uplifting of the surface of the globe. The columns which supported the cupola of the temple were taken to the Royal palace of Caserta and the statues and vases to the National Museum. This is the most important monument of Pozzuoli, above all remarkable for the richness of the marbles, its fine architecture and the artistic taste which ruled its construction. It appears to have been the Templee dedicated to Jupiter, and at the same time a Pantheon and Thermae. From thence, taking the road to BAJA, you see:

MONTE NUOVO whose existence dates only from the 30 September 1538. A volcanic explosion, lasting no less than 48 hours, whilst overwhelming a little village called Tre Pergole, raised this hill in its place. The summit still shows its origin.

The Lake Lucrino to the west of Monte Nuovo was partly overwhelmed by the same explosion, and close by is the:

Lake of Avernus from which Virgil makes Eneas descend into hell.

Agrippa, wishing to give a new port to the Roman fleets, made these two lakes communicate by means of a canal at which millions of slaves worked, but the same earthquake that created Monte Nuovo effaced every trace of their labours.

**The Grotta della Sibilla**, the baths of the same name, and the ruins of large baths, designated the Temple of Apollo and Mercury offer no real interest. They can be seen on applying to the Guardian to whom 1 franc is generally given for the entrance and 50 centimes for a torch. Here, as every where, strangers had better arrange the terms beforehand.

From the lake of Avernus, in going northwards, the highway is gained which leads to the:

**Arco Felice at Cuma** and the lake Fusaro. This town, which was situated on a hill close to the sea, occupies an exceptional place in history on account of its glories and its misfortunes. It is the most ancient Grecian colony and the ARCO FELICE was its principal entrance. A colossal torso of Jupiter in a sitting position was found in the building called the TEMPLE OF THE GIANTS. Other ruins such as temples, fortress walls etc. are scattered about this country.

**The lake Fusaro**, anciently ACHERUSIA, was famous for its oysters. On its banks are still seen ruins of villas and tombs, and a canal which the Romans constructed to lead to the sea.

From Fusaro you go to MISENO first passing through BAJA, where the Romans went for the summer season, then the village of BACOLI or BAULI, where the emperor Nero received his mother pretending to be reconciled to her in order the better to dissemble the odious plan he had made against her life,

**Le cento Camerelle**, or the LABYRINTH, or PRISONS OF NERO are in all probability only the cellars of one of his villas.

**La Piscina Mirabile**, a vast reservoir of

water for the use of the fleet and private persons. It is dug in the earth and 48 pillars support the roof. The large aqueduct Claudio joined this reservoir taking the waters from the province of Avellino nearly 100 kilometres distance.

**Cape Miseno,** rising to a peak above the sea was so called from Miseno, the trumpeter of Eneas, who, according to Virgil, was buried there.

The port of the same name, made in the reign of Augustus to give a refuge to the Roman fleet in the Mediterranean, comprised three basins of which the most famous is the MARE MORTO, also a crater of an ancient volcano. Between the Cape Miseno and the Monte Procida is:

**Miliscola** (Militum Schola) where the soldiers performed their manoeuvres. Several inscriptions found there tell us the names of those soldiers and sailors who carried off the prizes.

All this country supplies plentifully a good hydraulic cement known as *puzzolana*.

From Cape Miseno we can almost touch the two ISLANDS OF ISCHIA AND PROCIDA, so near are they to the continent. It is to be presumed that these two islands of volcanic origin once formed one. Ischia the *Pithecusa* of the ancients which is also the largest in the bay of Naples, deserves a special mention on account of its thermo mineral waters. It is a charming country where, during the summer, one can go as well for the waters as for a *villeggiatura*. A regular service of steamboats between this island and Naples adds to its animation, as visitors can go backwards and forwards twice a day. From the height of the Epomeo (Mount S.' Nicolas) is seen a beautiful view of the three gulfs o Gaeta, Naples and Salerno.

Returning from Miseno one can stop at:

**Baja** to see the TEMPLES OF DIANA, VENUS and MERCURY OR TRUGLIO, the BATHS OF TRITOLI (*hot mineral water*) and the STOVES OF NERO which are supposed to have communicated with these baths. In order to see the baths of Tritoli one must give the guide 50 centimes.

From Baja one returns to Naples through the town of Pozzuoli where, without leaving the carriage, one can see the pillars of the BRIDGE OF CALIGOLA.

The CATHEDRAL, situated on a height overlooking the town, occupies the site of a temple of Augustus of which the columns ornamenting the church formed a part. In the interior is the tomb of Pergolese.

Arrived at Bagnoli, instead of turning to the left you may drive towards the hill coasting the sea. The buildings on the right contain an important chemical manufactury. Half way up is the GROTTO OF SEJANO made by Lucullus to have a direct communication between his villa and the island of Nisida. This can be walked through all its length on giving a trifle to the guardian, and, on the other side, are to be seen the ruins of the VILLA OF LUCULLUS OR POLLIO. Not wishing to retrace your steps, tell the coachman, and, on mounting the hill by a little path which ends by the villa *Sans-Sauci*, you regain the carriage. From thence, you have only to return to Naples, following the graceful turns of the Pausilippo road whence is seen a splendid view of the town and bay.

After passing the barrier at the turning of the street is the Church of S.' Maria del Parto where is the TOMB OF THE POET SANNAZZARO.

Although we have treated this excursion

so that one would think it might be done in a day, we advice travellers to divided it into two, devoting the first day to the more important part, that is Pozzuoli, Baja, Cuma and the second to Agnano and Pausilippo.

The general price of a carriage to hold four, for the first excursion, is from 20 to 25 francs, for the second see the tariff.

The excursion to Baja cannot be made without refreshment on the way. Cold provisions therefore should be taken or one must be satisfied with lunch at the small restaurants in that neighbourhood, the price always being settled beforehand.

# THIRD PART

This third part shall be devoted to the churches and monuments, and to the environs of Naples which are charmingly attractive. We shall speak of all that the travaller should not omit seeing if he has a few days extra at his disposal.

**The Duomo or Cathedral** — This church, founded by Charles 1$^{st}$ of Anjou on the site of a temple dedicated to Neptune, was finished in the reign of Robert the great by Masuccio 1$^{st}$. Destroyed in 1456, by an earthquaque, it was rebuilt by Alphonso 1$^{st}$ of Aragon.

In the facade we admire the sculptures of the large door, due to Baboccio. The interior of the church is in the form of a latin cross with three naves divided by two ranks of pillars with columns of marble and oriental granite. The baptismal fonts in Egyptian basalt belonged to a pagan temple.

Above the large door are the TOMBS OF CHARLES 1$^{st}$ OF ANJOU and CHARLES MARTEL KING OF HUNGARY. Over the side doors TWO

PICTURES BY VASARI; the ceiling is ornamented with paintings by Santafede and do Forli. THE DOCTORS OF THE CHURCH, THE HOLY PATRONS OF THE TOWN AND THE TWELVE APOSTLES above the arches are by Luca Giordano; S.' CIRILLO and S.' CRISOSTOMO by Solimene.

In the Minutolo Chapel, constructed by Masuccio, is a TOMB OF A CARDINAL of this name by Baboccio. Another tomb, no less worthy of admiration, is that of Cardinal Carbone in the fourth chapel on the right, also due to Baboccio. Under the grand nave on the right is the CHAPEL OF S.' JANUARIUS where three times a year takes place, the famous miracle of the liquefaction of the blood of this celebrated martyr, and patron of the town of Naples. This chapel is closed by a BRONZE RAILING designed by Fansaga and the two statues placed on each side represent the Apostles S.' PETER and S.' PAUL.

Domenichino, charged with the decoration of the cupola, having completed the skylights as they are now seen, was going to commence the paintings of the roof when the envy and ill-will of his competitors made him renounce the work confided to his genius, and the cupola was finished after by Lanfranco.

The paintings reproduce the principal facts in the life of S.' Januarius, executed by the same Domenichino who did the altar pictures excepting those of the second and third, due, the one to Spagnoletto, and the other to the Chevalier Massimo. The chief altar in porphyry was designed by Solimene.

In the Sacristy are real chefs d' oeuvre of Luca Giordano, besides a rich collection of offerings called the treasure of S.' Januarius to which nearly all the conquerors of Naples have largely contributed in the hope of flattering the clergy and people.

To explain the value of these treasures it suffices to say that the mitre of the Saint contains 3,690 precious stones such as diamands, emeralds, rubies etc.

On leaving the Chapel of S.' Januarius you go to the Sacristy of the Church where is seen on the wall at the right a painting on wood representing Pope Innocent 4th in the act of giving the red hat, for the first time, to the Cardinals, symbolising by this colour the blood they should be ready to shed for the greatness and safety of the Church.

In the same Sacristy are several objects of art of great price amongst which is a picture by Perugino, very badly restored, representing the Virgin and Angels. Notice also in the crypt of S.' Januarius the Chapel of the Carafas d' Andria with beautiful sculptures, and a statue of Cardinal Oliviero Carafa, which artists attribute to Michael-Angelo Naccarini.

A little door opposite the chapel of S.' Januarius leads to the Church of S.' Restituta an ancient Basilica founded in 334 on the ruins of a temple dedicated to Apollo. The vaults are decorated with Byzantine mosaics of the 13th century.

Note. *The treasure of S.' Januarius can only be visited with the permission of the President of the deputation of S.' Januarius, charged with administering the patrimony of the chapel.*

**The Church of the Gerolomini** was built at the expense of the Fathers of the Oratory on the plans of Denis Bartolomeo excepting the front designed by Denis Lazzari. The architect Fuga being charged to make this facade to suit the interior of the Church recovered it with marble adding the two steeples. The Church is richly decorated with paintings by masters such as Corenzio, Solimene and

Giordano. A large fresco, by this last is above the great door. The Sacristy is even more interesting to visit than the Church, it contains a large number of canvasses by Guido Reni, Tintoretto, Bassano, Spagnoletto, the Chevalier Arpino, Domenichino etc.

The philosopher Giovan Battista Vico is buried in this Church and a simple stone on the right of the chief altar reminds us of this great man.

**S.' Giovanni a Carbonara** — This Church has many admirable tombs, amongst which we notice that of the king Ladislas and another of Ser Gianni Caracciolo a favourite of queen Joan $2^{nd}$. In the chapel of this last named, notice the frescoes by Leonardo Bisucci a Milanese, and pupil of Giotto. These two tombs are by Ciccione. In the sacristy are fifteen frescoes by Vasari.

**The Annunziata** destroyed by fire in 1757 was rebuilt, 25 years after, with even more richness, on the plans of Vanvitelli. Its architecture is very fine and the cupola deserves special attention. The sacristy is adorned with beautiful paintings by Corenzio, and round the walls is a cabinet in carved wood by Giovanni da Nola in his youth. In the

1ˢᵗ chapel notice a fine picture on the altar by F. Curia depicting the presentation in the temple.

S.' **Domenico** is built in gothic style on vast dimensions. Amongst the paintings look at the following:

A VIRGIN WITH THE INFANT JESUS, *school of Giotto.*

AN ANNUNCIATION, *Venetian school.*

A SCOURGING, *School of Caravaggio.*

A S.' JOSEPH BY GIORDANO; and in the sacristy:

A TRINITY BY SOLIMENE.

Look also at the monuments on both sides.

At the back of this Church rises a somewhat barocco Obelisk surmounted by a statue of the Saint. It was begun by Fansaga, and finished by Vaccaro in 1737. The works necessary for its foundation led to the discovery of the ancient gate Cumana or Puteolana.

**Chapel of S.' Severo** private property of the prince of this name. This little chapel which is situated by the side of that of S.' Domenico encloses many tombs and statues worth notice, rather for the execution of the work than as pieces of sculpture:

1ˢᵗ the tomb of Antonio di Sangro, ornamented with a fine statue (by Queiroli) symbolical of DISILLUSION represented as a man wrapped in a net.

2$^{nd}$ A statue (by Corradini) representing CHASTITY wrapped in a veil.

3$^{rd}$ The REDEEMER, dead, laid on a base of porphyry, by Giuseppe Sammartino.

**Santa Chiara** was built in 1313 in the reing of Robert of Anjou. Observe the tombs of the kings of Naples, and behind the chief altar, a monument erected to the same Robert from the designs of Masuccio 1$^{st}$. This Church was anciently decorated with paintings by Giotto; a picture of the Virgin on one of the altars on the right, is all that remains of this master. The paintings of the ceiling are much esteemed and that in the centre is by Chevalier Conca.

The large tower serving as belfrey to the Church is by Masuccio 2$^{nd}$. It should have five stages representing the different orders of architecture. Never having been completed it has only three; the Tuscan, the Doric and the Jonic.

**The Gesù Nuovo** built in 1584 is rich in fine marbles. The cheif door is a handsome work of the period. The two columns supporting the broken arch are more recent. This Church is decorated with frescoes by Solimene, Corenzio, Stanzioni and Vaccaro. The skylights, and the cupola, are by Lanfranco; the fresco on the great door is by Solimene, and there are other paintings by Giordano, Battistello, Spagnoletto, Siciliani etc.

The chief altar remade some years ago is rich in porphyry, agate and jasper. The bronze bas reliefs are the work of the sculptor Cali, and the statue of the Conception is by Busciolano. Before this Church is an Obelisk erected by a Jesuit in 1747 which has a certain beauty in its details.

**S.' Paolo** in the street of the Tribunali is raised on the site of a temple dedicated to Castor and Pollux.

The two handsome columns adorning the great door belonged to that ancient temple. The Church, having been destroyed, was rebuilt on the plans of a monk and richly decorated with marbles and pictures by Corenzio, Solimene, Stanzioni and other authors celebrated in the Neapolitan school.

**S.' Lorenzo** nearly opposite S.' Paolo dates from 1266, and was founded in commemoration of a victory gained by Charler 1st of

Anjou over king Manfred. Its architecture, in the modified gothic style, is by Maglione, a pupil of Nicolas Pisano. Observe, above all, the extreme end behind the chief altar and the arch of the great nave. This Church contains fine statues amongst which, those of S.' Francis, S.' Lawrence and S.' Anthony, as also the bas reliefs of the chief altar all by Giovanni da Nola, and on the back of this altar are fine sculptures and monuments in mosaics and reliefs. In 1343 Petrarch lived in the adjoining convent, and it was in this Church that Boccaccio saw for the first time the beautiful princess he rendered so famous in his novels under the name of Fiammetta. In leaving, notice on the right the tomb of Giovan Battista della Porta.

**The Church of the Incoronata** in the strada Medina was so called because there took plece the marriage and coronation of queen Giovanna 1", niece of king Robert, with her cousin Louis of Tarant. It contains several frescoes by Giotto and his pupils restored by no clever hand.

**S.' Giacomo degli Spagnuoli** in the piazza of the Municipio contains the handsome monument erected to D. Pietro di Toledo and his wife and fine pictures of Bernard de Lama, Marco da Siena, and other celebrated artists.

**The Church S.' Severino** of very fine architecture has, in the choir, the large frescoes by Corenzio representing the pomp of the Benedictine order, and others by the same author on the walls and below the vault of the cross. The paintings of the large nave and the picture above the great door are by F. Mura, those over the little door by Perugino. The Redeemer on the cross and others are attributed to Marco da Siena. The statue on the tomb of V. Carafa is by Naccarini. The tombs of the three brothers S. Severino are by Merliani.

Other Churches, such as Monteoliveto, S.' Maria la Nuova, S.' Marcellino, S.' Maria di Constantinopoli, Donna Regina, S.' Agostino della Zecca, S.' Caterina a Formella and S.' Maria degli Angeli at Pizzofalcone, enclose many artistic beauties to which a connaisseur might pleasantly devote some days.

---

**The Royal Palace** was built in 1669 after the plans of Domenico Fontana. The handsome front showing in its three stages, three kinds of architecture leads us to appreciate the progress of art raising itself from its fallen state. Besides the state apartments, other rooms contain several pictures and we observe two portraits one by Rembrandt, the other by Velasquez, and many more by Flemish authors, also the pictures by Titian and the frescoes by Corenzio.

The paintings in the chapel are by modern artists and the part of the palace lately restored is decorated with frescoes by Neapolitan painters, Guerra, Maldarelli, Marsigli and Cammarano.

The balconies of the south side open on a large terrace from which there is a beautiful wiew of the bay.

Note. *Cards of admittance are given for visiting the palace from the office of the General Superintendant of the Royal house, one has only to apply to the Concierge of the Palace if not already provided with a permission through his Consul. It is the same as regards all the other crown properties.*

**The Theatre of San Carlo** is attached to the royal palace. A stranger should not leave Naples without spending an evening at this theatre, to see the vastity of the hall, its decorations, and listen to its harmonious sound.

**The Castel Nuovo** opposite the municipal palace, founded in 1283, by Charles 1ˢᵗ of Anjou, was the residence of the kings of this dynasty, of that of Aragon, and of the Spanish viceroys.

Alphonso 1ˢᵗ of Aragon enlarged it by adding the towers. Pietro di Toledo built the remparts and Charles 3ʳᵈ of Bourbon gave it its present form. The fino triumphal arch whose gates have been valued at several millions of francs, was built to celebrate the entry of king Alphonso 1ˢᵗ. The statues and bas-reliefs, admirable both in design and execution, are the work of Neapolitan and other Italian artists. Entering on the right is the Armoury once the hall reserved for the receptions of the kings of Naples, and in the inner court of the barracks is the Church of S.' Barbara or S.' Sebastian with Corinthian front enclosing a picture attributed to Van-Dych. To visit this Hall one must be provided with a permission from the Minister of War, and on leaving the

Church it is customary to give 50 cent. to the guardian.

**The University** — Nothing can be positively asserted as to the origin of the University of Naples. The only thing certain is that it existed at the beginning of the 13th century and that the emperor Frederick 2nd in 1224 wishing to enlarge and improve it, developed it to that point to deserve all the merit of a founder rather than that of a simple reformer. The University has occupied the present building since 1777. It possesses a library containing 25,000 volumes among which are most rare editions, collections of natural history and cabinets of physics and chemistry. The library is open to the public daily from 9 o'clock a. m. till 3.

**The Botanical Garden** at the end of the strada Foria is a dependence of the University. Its foundation dates from 1809, and besides a rich collection of plants of all kinds it contains four herb gardens, autographs of the most celebreted botanists, instruments for microscopic observations, and a library.

**The National Library** (see the National Museum).

**The Brancacciana Library** in the small square of S.' Angelo a Nilo close to the University, was given to the public by Cardinal Brancaccio. It contains 70,000 volumes and 7,000 manuscripts. Open every afternoon.

**The Library of S.' Giacomo** in the strada Concezione a Toledo, is also open daily from 6 to 10 p. m. It is composed of the private books of king Ferdinand $2^{nd}$.

**The Library of the Gerolomini** opposite the Duomo is open from 9 to 11 a. m., contains 18,000 volumes among which is the celebrated edition of Seneca, of the $14^{th}$ century, decorated with miniatures by Zingaro.

**The Grand Archives** of the kingdom of the two Sicilies occupy three cloisters and several rooms in the convent of S.' Severino and Sossio near the University. The third of these cloisters is particularly noticeable for a marble portico and statues which adorn the little garden. Among the rooms on the ground floor, the handsomest are the two called the Chapter and the Cenacle with frescoes by Corenzio. The Archives enclose a rich collection of parchments and historical documents commencing from the $17^{th}$ century.

**Royal Academy** *of Archeology, Literature and Fine Arts.*

**Pontaniana Academy**, for mathematical natural and political sciences, history, literature and the fine arts.

**Institution for Encouragement** of the natural sciences, economics and technologies.

**Institution of the Fine Arts** in strada Costantinopoli.

---

Naples is endowed with many beneficent establishments chiefly due to private charity. We note the principal:

**The Large Hospital called Incurabili** for all except chronic illnesses.

**The Hospital della Pace** for fever patients.

**The Hospital dei Pellegrini** for the wounded.

**The Asylum of S.¹ Giuseppe e Lucia** for the blind.

**The Annunziata** for foundlings.

**The Clinical Hospital of Gesù e Maria.**

**Large Asylum for the poor** of both sexes, commonly called Reclusorio, founded in 1751, in the reign of Charles 3rd, on the plans of Fuga. All the young pupils, girls or boys, are taught a trade.

**The Cemitery** (Campo-Santo) to the East of the town. It is attained by the beautiful road in continuation of the strada Foria. Its fine situation, and handsome monuments, induce us to bring it under the visitors notice. It is a nice drive for which a carriage had better be taken by the hour according to the tariff, but an arrangement should be made with the driver before starting.

**The Palace of Capodimonte** is the summer residence of the king and the princes. There is a collection of pictures of the Neapolitan and Northern Italy schools, two pictures of Camuccini representing the death of Cesar, and that of Virginia, and a Judith by Benvenuto. Special catalogues are in each room. It contains besides a collection of ancient arms amongst which the helmet and shield of Roger the Norman, and the sword which Louis 14$^{th}$ presented to Philip of Anjou. One of the rooms of the state apartements is covered with porcelain of the old Capodimonte manufacture, now very rare. The park is very pretty and strangers will be pleased to take a turn in it, and for greater convenience permission is given also for carriages to enter.

For this excursion the same as for the

cemitery, a carriage by the hour had better be taken and the price settled beforehand as both places are beyond the limits of the town.

Returning from Capodimonte and arriving at the Museum turn to the right and by the Via Salvator Rosa and Corso Vittorio Emanuele you get home after having enjoyed a nice drive with beautiful points of scenery.

**The Camaldoli** situated on the highest of the hills surrounding Naples, from which the most splendid panorama is seen; is one of the best excursions that can be made to the environs of the town. Donkeys can be hired for 1 fr. 50 cent. at the commencement of the strada Salvator Rosa and a trifle besides is given to the guide.

Carriages can also go as far as the village of Antignano (see the tariff) and there one either hires donkeys or goes on foot up to the convent. In any way the excursion takes four hours.

There is nothing remarkable in the Convent or Church. A franc is generally given to the guardian who shows the Belvedere, the chief aim of the excursion, is the extensive view of the gulfs of Naples, Pozzuoli and Gaeta, and the entire plain of the province of Terra di Lavoro.

**Caserta** is 45 minutes from Naples by rail. The Royal Palace built in the reign of Charles 3rd, on the plans of Vanvitelli, must be seen; much time is needed to visit this immense bulding therefore we note the most remarkable parts of it. It has four large interior courts united by grand pillars which support the whole building. Let us give it a glance, standing in the centre, which is striking; after which we will notice the grand staircase, composed of 117 marble steps the greatest part in one single block. On the first floor is the chapel decorated with a profusion of marbles, lapis-lazzuli and gilding; next the theatre supported by 16 columns taken from the temple of Serapis near Pozzuoli. This is one of the most magnificent and largest palaces, being 35 metres high and nearly 200 wide. The front has 240 windows. Attached to the palace is the park whose chief attraction is its fountains. The basin and cascade are laid out in perspective of wide extent, it is nearly 2 kilometres from the gate of the palace to the foot of the cascade. All the waters arrive there after a long course passing close to Maddaloni by an acqueduct of three orders of arcades. It would be well to obtain from the Royal Palace at Naples, a permission to drive through the park. If a little rest is required we indicate the:

Hotel Vittoria, near the railway station and the Royal Palace, with private apartments, dining room; table d'hôte or dinner a la carte. Also board by the week. The entrance is by the garden.

**The Ascension of Vesuvius** though very fatiguing is too classical an excursion for a stranger to omit. One should therefore make this ascent, and to do so with comfort and pleasure, choose a fine winter's day and descend at sun set, or a fine summer morning, and arrive there at sun rise. We will not give the history of all the eruptions which have taken place at different periods, nor even of the changes in shape which this mountain has undergone. This last eruption of the month of April (1872) has given the most imposing and terrible spectacle. The celebreted pine discribed by Plynio was reproduced in all its truthful grandeur. The mountain after this has still considerably changed in shape; the valley separating Vesuvius from Somma called *atrio del cavallo*, and the other separating the astronomical observatory are nearly filled up with lava.

The ascension is not dangerous if the directions of the guides be followed and the crater not too closely approached. To get there one must go from Naples to Resina where guides are to be got. One is sufficient for several persons and the usual remuneration is 5 fr. The same price is paid for a horse with 1 franc to the man who takes charge of it whilst ascending the cone.

As to refreshments on the way, it is almost as indispensable here as elsewhere that one be provided with eatables from Naples, also to avoid, as much as possible, the buying any at Resina, or on the mountain, for all is exceedingly dear. Refuse also any offers of help and attend to the guide's explanations.

**Castellammare** — One hour by rail from Naples, is a town noted for its mineral waters and healthy situation. It is frequented during the summer by many strangers, and has good hotels, furnished houses and apartments. We here give some addresses:

HOTEL ROYAL near the railway station.

HOTEL DE LA GRANDE BRETAGNE upon the hill of Quisisana near the forest.

Pension Anglaise kept by Miss Baker near the station and 10 minutes from the town on the road leading to Gragnano.

In all these establishments the service is comfortable, the food very good, and the air most healthful. The mineral waters of the country can be had at the wish of the visitors.

The town was built on the site of the ancient one of Stabia destroyed by Vesuvius at the same time as Pompei. The castle fort which gave its name is now a ruin and was built in the reign of Frederick $2^{nd}$, in the $13^{th}$ century.

The forest of Quisisana and the Mount Coppola is a beautiful walk or ride. The price of a donkey there and back is at most 2 fr. Behind Castellamare rises Mount Santangelo 1,452 m. above the level of the sea. Its ascension is made in four hours, paying 5 fr. horse and guide. From the top of this mountain there is an admirable view, extending on one side to the mountains of the Abrusses, and, on the other, to the Calabrias. The view is finest from the high point on which the chapel stands, where you should tell the guide to take you. The time for return should be calculated.

From Castellamare you go to:

**Sorrento** passing through Vico Equense, whose cathedral encloses the tomb of Gaetano Filangieri. A carriage with two horses costs 5 francs, with one 3 francs. Sorrento was Tasso's country where his house is shewn. In summer one can go by steamer or one of the sailing boats stationed near the port. Crossing by these last costs 1 fr.; but we warn ladies that the company is often far from agreable.

Sorrento also has good hotels, furnished appartments and boarding houses, viz:

Hotel de la Syrene

Hotel du Tasso
   (*kept by the brothers Gargiulo*).

Hotel Villa-Strongoli

Hotel Villa-Nardi
   (*kept by G. Tramontano*).

Hotel de la Grande-Bretagna
   (*kept by the brothers Fiorentino*).

Hotel Rispoli in the piazza del Tasso.

All these hotels are surrounded by beautiful gardens and look on the sea. They have private paths by which visitors can descend either to bathe, or to enjoy a row, or go for an excursion in one of the boats which the proprietors of these hotels have always ready for their use.

Travallers may dine either a la carte or at the table d'hôte, and nothing is neglected that can conduce to their comfort either as to the service or the cuisine.

There are also carriages for any excursions, and donkeys and horses for ascending the neighbouring mountains.

The delightful excursion to Deserto takes nearly three hours. On donkeys costs 1 fr. 50 cent. or 2. fr. and 25 cent. to the guide. From the roof of a little convent which is on the Deserto, a fine view is seen of the gulf of Salerno. The donkey guides are always ready with pretexts to prevent travellers stopping at the convent with the aim of returning quickly to Sorrento; we give the warning in order that travellers may make the excursion at their ease and pay no attention to the observations made them.

Several establishments of cabinet work and mosaic in wood exist in Sorrento, amongst others the most recommended are those of:

LOUIS AND ALBERICO GARGIULÓ father and son.

MICHEL GRANDVILLE and

Joseph Gargiulo.

All these manufacturers have obtained prizes at the Exhibitions of London and Paris.

Now in Sorrento is the Casino called Club of Sorrento open to the public in the day time and the evening.

The terms of admission are:

| | | |
|---|---|---|
| Per annum . . . | francs | 70 |
| 6 Months. . . . . | » | 50 |
| Month. . . . . | » | 10 |
| Week . . . . . | » | 3 |
| Day . . . . . . | » | 1 |

N.B. Ladies accompanied half price.

**The Island of Capri** — Noted for its wines, is not less celebrated on account of the stay made there by the Emperors Augustus and Tiberius. The price of a four-oared boat, from Sorrento, going and returning, is 10 francs and 1 fr. extra to the sailors. For a two oared boat, 6 to 8 fr. The island has only two villages, Capri and Anacapri, and good hotels, restaurants and boarding houses; we mention the principal ones:

Hotel Tiberio kept by A. Ross is a very good hotel, pleasantly situated, and looking over the gulf. Here one finds all possible comforts combined with moderate price.

Hotel Quisisana kept by M.rs Clark. Large and good hotel well situated, with terraces from which there is a very fine view; moderate prices, english and french spoken.

Hotel de France kept by Louis Astarita. Pension at moderate price.

Hotel Vittoria kept by M. Pagano. Central position, clean and the services good. It is frequented chiefly by artists.

The last named village is attained by mounting 536 steps cut in the rock.

It is hardly necessary to say there are plenty of Roman ruins in this island. The most part belong to twelve Augustan-Tiberian villas and take their names from twelve divinities.

For excursions, a donkey by the day is 3 francs and a trifle to its leader who acts also as guide.

The excursion to Capri is really only interesting for seeing:

**The Grotta Azzurra** — In this grotto all is blue excepting objects in the water which have a beautiful silvery appearance. Boatmen are always there, ready to throw themselves in, and show this astonishing effect on their bodies. 50 centimes is quite sufficient remuneration. This grotto was discovered in 1822 and is 53 metres long and 32 broad with a roof formed of stalactites. The entrance is rather difficult and even dangerous sometimes on account of the East and North winds. The best time for seeing it is from 10 in the morning to 1 o' clock in the afternoon because the weather is generally calm at that time of the day.

As the last excursion we propose that to:

**Poestum** at 50 kilometres from Salerno; was founded about 600 years before the christian era, by the emigrants from Stabia. As the railway does not go there we think the best plan would be to go to Salerno the evening before, stay all night and go to Poestum next day. Salerno is a somewhat important town and if arriving before night fall one would have time to visit its Cathedral of historical interest. Its construction dates from 1084. For lodging we propose the:

Hotel d'Angleterre agreably situated in the new street of the Marina having a view over the gulf. Visitors will find in this hotel all the advantages of a large establishment, cleanliness, comfort and exactitude in the service at prices relatively moderate.

From Salerno to Poestum the ordinary price of a carriage with four seats is from

25 to 30 francs, and the excursion does not take less than 11 hours, 8 for going and returning, 3 for seeing the ruins. Nothing can be got to eat at Poestum so one should take lunch, and eat it on arriving. The marshes surrounding these ruins give exhalations in the summer which produce *malaria*.

A party of not fewer then sixteen persons can make this excursion by way of Viètri and Amalfi, visiting the beautiful coast of that name. 50 francs for each person covers all expenses. The party leaves Naples every Wednesday morning; omnibusses starting from the door of the hotel Vittoria at 7 $^1/_2$ a. m. They proceed by rail to Vietri, where carriages wait to convey them to Amalfi, and having lunched, they proceed to Salerno for dinner at 6 p. m. Here they will spend the night and take an early train on the following morning for Battipaglia, where they will find carriages to convey them to Poestum. In either way this excursion is made travellers must try to return to Battipaglia in time to catch the last train to Naples.

Further informations can be had at the office of MM. Cerulli and C.º N. 29 Vittoria.

At Poestum are the remains of Grecian architecture which are perhaps the most complete existing. First the TEMPLE OF NEPTUNE formed with a portico supported outside by 36 fluted doric columns, and inside by 16, surmounted by a second colonnade supporting the roof. The greater part of these columns are of travertin in good condition, yellowed by time. This temple, of exceptional beauty, is also the most ancient monument of Grecian architecture. THE BASILICA and TEMPLE OF CERES, the AMPHITEATRE, the THEATRE and some other ruins are only of a secondary interest.

We have said it would be as well to sleep at Salerno and make the Poestum excursion next day, and we must add it would be worthwhile to leave Naples in the morning and stop some hours at:

**La Cava**, an ancient Tyrrhenian town, to visit the Benedectine Convent whose foundation dates from the 11th century. It is situated on a hill which is reached on donkeys. The Church contains many remarkable tombs among which we notice those of the Abbot S.ᵗ Alferius, Queen Sybilla and Gregory 8th. The organ is considered one of the finest in Italy. Nothing however equals the importance of the Archives of this Convent and to give an idea of them it suffices to say that the catalogue alone comprehends 8 volumes. Amongst the documents are the CODEX LEGUM LONGOBARDORUM of 1004, and the VOLGATA LATINA of the 7th century, besides a large number of valuable parchments and manuscripts. These archives are only to be seen in the morning.

The town of La Cava is much liked by strangers and Neapolitans who willingly make their summer stay there.

At this point we think we can leave the traveller. It might be objected that a country so dear to the ancient rulers of the world whose beauty is proverbial should offer more excursions either historically interesting or simply agreeable. To this we answer the POCKET-GUIDE has omitted nothing, but that it has merely avoided taking strangers to such parts where without a flow of imagination they would experience disappointment. Those who have followed this Guide in all its excursions should now know enough of the country, whose language is easily learned, to be able to gain other information for themselves.

# FOURTH PART

## ADDRESSES

---

### ARTISTS STUDIOS

Ch.' Palizzi — N. 37 Strada della Pace.
Commd.' Morelli — N. 37 Strada della Pace.
Ch.' Maldarelli — Albergo dei Poveri.
Ch.' V. Marinelli — N. 40 S. Margarita a Fonseca.
Ch.' Mancinelli — Instituto of Fine Arts — Strada Costantinopoli.
Ch.' A. Licata — N. 14 Monte di Dio.
Giovanni Ponticelli — N. 64 Piazza Cavour 1" floor.
Gennaro Guglielmi — Corso Vittorio Emanuele near the convent of S. Pasquale.
Cesare Uva landscape painter — N. 265 Riviera di Chiaia.
Edoardo Tofano — N. 37 Strada della Pace.
Del Bono — N. 85 Mergellina.
Boschetto — Mergellina Palazzo Barbaja.

Miola — N. 20 Largo Marinelli a Magnocavallo.
Del Re — N. 35 Salita Stella.
Sagliano — N. 45 Largo Mater Dei.
Parise — N. 46 Vico Lungo Avvocata.
Carrillo — N. 7 S. Carlo alle Mortelle.
Consalvo Carelli — N. 13 Strada Bisignano.
Gabriele Smargiassi — N. 27 Via Mandella Gaetana.
Giacinto Gigante — Salita Due porte.
Cortese — N. 6 Posillipo.
Russo — S. Andrea delle Dame.
Netti — N. 5 Arco Mirelli.
Petruccelli — Capodimonte Palazzo Tourner.
Caracciolo — Palazzo Francavilla a Chiaia.
Nacciarone — Corso Vittorio Emmanuele, Palazzo Mancone.
Altamura — N. 185 Riviera di Chiaia.

## NEAPOLITAN ARTIST'S GALLERY
### 37 Strada Pace a Chiaia.

Oil Paintings, Water-Colours, Drawings, Engravings, Works of Art.
The exibition is open every day from 11 to 4. Free entrance.

## SCULPTORS STUDIOS

Ch.' Tito Angelini — Albergo dei Poveri.
Ch.' Tommaso Solari — Strada Costantinopoli in the Instituto of Fine Arts.
Stanislao Lista — Largo S. Aniello alla Strada Costantinopoli.
Francesco Liberti — Albergo dei Poveri.
O. Buccino — In the Villa garden a Chiaja.
Pietro Masulli — N. 64 Piazza dei Martiri.
Ernest Calì — N. 269 Riviera di Chiaia.

## WOOD CARVERS

Franceschi — Strada Nuova Capodimonte close by the Casa operaja.
Ottajano — N. 27 Strada Costantinopoli..
Pagano — Corso Vittorio Emanuele Palazzo Montemiletto.

## ANTIQUARIANS

Vincenzo Barone — N. 6 Strada Trinità Maggiore.
Pasquale Janniello — N. 92-93 Strada Costantinopoli and 11 Strada Sapienza 2ᵈ floor.

Francesco Scognamiglio — N. 97 Strada Costantinopoli.
James — N. 13 Strada della Pace.

## PHOTOGRAPHS

Lejeune — N. 47 Strada Cavallerizza a Chiaja.
Arena — N. 7 Strada della Pace e Piazza dei Martiri.
Ferretti — N. 23 Chiatamone.
Grillet — N. 6 Chiatamone.

## PHOTOGRAPH SELLERS
### and objects of fine arts

Scala — N. 42 Strada S.ta Catarina a Chiaja.
Amodio — N. 3 Strada S.ta Catarina a Chiaia.
Sommer — N. 5 Strada S.ta Catarina a Chiaja.

## MANUFACTORIES
### of articles in terra-cotta in the antique style

Giustiniani — N. 20 Strada del Gigante.
Mollica — N. 27 Strada S.ta Lucia.

## STATIONERS

ENGLISH STATIONARY FROM PARKINS AND GOTTO — N. 59 Piazza dei Martiri.
SCIELZO — N. 206 Strada di Chiaja.
MAZZARELLA — N. 223 Via Roma.
MIGLIORATO — N. 273 Via Roma.
TIPALDI — N. 51 Strada Montoliveto.

## BOOKSELLERS

DETKEN ET ROCHOLL — Piazza of Plebiscito.
DURA — N. 40 Strada S. Carlo. Speciality for ancient books.
PELLERANO — N. 60 Strada di Chiaja.
PERRUCCHETTI — N. 110 Strada di Chiaja.
DURA — N. 10 Strada di Chiaja. Foreign library, photografs and objects of fine art.

## LITHOGRAPHS

RICHTER AND C.º — Under the portico of S. Francesco di Paola.
STEEGER — N. 22 Via Gennaro Serra.

GIANNINI — Typographic Establishment N. 31 Via Museo Nazionale with succursal Strada Cisterna dell' Olio N. 5.

## JEWELLERS

TAVASSI — N. 250 Strada di Chiaja.
FRANCONERI — N. 233 Via Roma.
FECARROTTA — N. 278-279 Via Roma.

## WATCH MAKERS

RICCIO — N. 47 Piazza S.' Ferdinando.
TAFURI — N. 274 Via Roma.

## WORKERS IN CORAL AND LAVA

FRATELLI ERRICO — N. 39-40 Strada S.$^{ta}$ Caterina a Chiaja.
CASALTA E MORABITO — N. 60 Piazza dei Martiri.
BOLTEN — N. 58 1$^{st}$ floor Piazza dei Martiri.
GAGLIARDI — N. 7 Piazza della Vittoria.
BOLLA — N. 25 Strada del Gigante.
ANNUNZIATA — N. 24 Strada del Gigante.
MERLINO — N. 18-19 Strada del Gigante.

## WORKERS IN TORTOISE SHELL

F. LABRIOLA — Piazza della Vittorta at the entrance of the Villa garden.

TAGLIAFERRI — N. 43 Strada S.ᵗᵃ Catarina a Chiaja.
M. LABRIOLA — N. 69 Strada S.ᵗᵃ Catarina a Chiaja.
FERRANTE E Rosso — N. 50 Strada S. Carlo.

## CAMEO CUTTERS

LAUDICINO — N. 268 Riviera di Chiaja.
STELLA — N. 9 Strada Pace.

## SORRENTO WORK

N. 43 Strada S.ᵗᵃ Catarina a Chiaja.

## GLOVE MANUFACTORY

PELLERANO — N. 70 Strada S.ᵗᵃ Caterina a Chiaja.
CUOSTA — N. 137 Strada di Chiaja.
BOUDILLON — N. 202 Strada di Chiaja.
F.ᴸᴸᴵ AMENDOLA — N. 244 Strada di Chiaja.
F. CREMONESI AND C.º — N. 50 Piazza S. Ferdinando.

## NAPLES SILKS

MANUFACTORY OF S.ᵗ LEUCIO NEAR CASERTA DEPOT AND SALE — N. 67 Strada dei Fiorentini.

## CATANIAN SILKS

GIUSEPPE AUTERI e FRAGALÀ — N. 288 Via Roma.

## MILLINERS AND DRESS MAKER

A. POMA — N. 195-196 Strada di Chiaja.
JOURDAN — N. 209 1$^{st}$ floor Strada di Chiaja.
MAISON RICCO — N. 8-9 Strada S$^{ta}$ Catarina a Chiaja.

## BOOT MAKERS

BURRINGTON — N. 57 Piazza dei Martiri.
FINOJA — N. 53-54 Strada Alabardieri.
BALDELLI — N. 50 Strada di Chiaia.
CHAUSSURES DE PARIS — N. 256 1$^{st}$ floor Via Roma.

## TAILORS

J. Lennon — N. 2 Strada S.ta Catarina a Chiaja.
Mackenzie — N. 51 Piazza dei Martiri.

## HAT-MAKERS

Mammolino — N. 258 Via Roma.
De Francesco — N. 181 Via Roma.

## UMBRELLA-MAKERS

De Martino — N. 211 Strada di Chiaja.
J. Gilardini — N. 335-336 Via Roma.

## HAIRDRESSERS

Zempt — N. 6 Strada S.ta Catarina a Chiaja.
Carafa — N. 232 1st floor Strada di Chiaja.

## WINE MERCHANTS

Pasquale Scala — N. 136 Strada di Chiaja.
Rouff — N. 146 Strada di Chiaja.

SCALA GIUSEPPE — N. 42 Via Concezione a Toledo.
FEROCE — N. 64 Piazza del municipio.

## PASTRYCOOK

BOULANGERIE ET PATISSERIE FRANCAISES — N. 51-52 Piazza S. Ferdinando.

## CONFECTIONERS

DE ANGELIS — N. 247 Via Roma.
D' ALBERO — N. 218-219 Via Roma.
F. FERRONI — N. 3-4 Strada S$^{ta}$ Brigida.
ENGLISH GROCER — Piazza della Vittoria and Riviera di Chiaja.

## CHARCUTIERS

GIUSEPPE PAUTASSO — N. 54 Piazza S. Ferdinando.
RAVEL FRÈRES — N. 224 Via Roma.

## MANUFACTURY OF ARMS

Bodeo et Carrara — N. 61-62 Strada di Chiaja.
Izzo — N. 33 Strada S. Carlo.
Mazza — N. 36 Piazza del Municipio.

## FURNITURE AND DECORATION
### of appartments

Rempt — N. 1 Strada S.ᵗᵃ Catarina a Chiaja.
Filippo Haas e figli — N. 225-226 Via Roma.
Levera — N. 350 Via Roma.
Bonniot, Robiony et Franceschi — N. 371-372 Via Roma.
Solei, Hebert et C.º — N. 27 Str. S. Brigida.
Fabric of the Fibreno for paper hangings N. 274-275 Via Roma.
Fabric of coloured and opaque glasses — Benvenuti N. 25 strada S. Brigida.

## WORK IN MARROCCO LEATHER
### and in linen cloth

O. Forti and C.º — N. 51 Strada di Chiaja.

## CHEMISTS

Zofra — N. 62 Strada S.$^{ta}$ Catarina a Chiaja.
Valentino e Saggese — Pharmacie francaise et anglaise — N. 31 Largo Garofolo.
A. Petriccione — Pharmacie Anglo-Napolitaine — N. 118.
E. Berncastel — Pharmacie Prussienne — N. 7 Strada S. Francesco di Paola.
Kernot — N. 14 Strada S. Carlo.
Scarpitti — N. 325 Via Roma.
Dragone — Homeopatic pharmacy — N. 188 Strada di Chiaja.

# INDEX

PREFACE.
. INTRODUCTION.

| | | |
|---|---|---|
| **First Part** — Arrival....... | pag. | 10 |
| Tariffs........... | » | 10–13 |
| Hotels and Boarding-houses... | » | 14–15 |
| Bath-Establishments...... | » | 16 |
| Restaurants and Cafès restaurants. | » | 16–17 |
| Post offices.......... | » | 17 |
| Thelegraphs......... | » | 18 |
| Bankers........... | » | 18 |
| Consuls........... | » | 19–20 |
| Police office......... | » | 20 |
| Reading-rooms........ | » | 20 |
| Protestant Churches...... | » | 21 |
| Language Masters....... | » | 22 |
| Music Masters......... | » | 22 |
| Fabric and hire of pianos.... | » | 23 |
| Music Editors......... | » | 23 |
| Institutions for young ladies... | » | 23 |
| » for young gentlemen. | » | 23 |
| Theatres........... | » | 24 |
| Clubs............ | » | 24–26 |
| Doctors........... | » | 26–28 |
| **Second Part** — Few hours stroll.. | » | 29–32 |
| National Museum....... | » | 32–65 |

| | |
|---|---|
| Certosa of S. Martino . . . . . . » | 65–67 |
| Castle of S. Elmo . . . . . . . » | 68 |
| Excursions at Pompei . . . . . » | 68–74 |
| » Herculaneum . . . . » | 74 |
| » Pozzuoli—Daja—Cumae » | 74–84 |
| » Pausilippo . . . . . » | 84–85 |
| **Third Part**—Churches and Monuments » | 86–95 |
| Royal palace of Naples . . . . . » | 95–96 |
| » of Capodimonte . . . » | 101 |
| Theatre of S. Carlo . . . . . . . » | 96 |
| Castel-Nuovo . . . . . . . . . » | 97 |
| University . . . . . . . . . . » | 98 |
| Botanical Garden . . . . . . » | 98 |
| Libraries . . . . . . . . . . » | 99 |
| Grand Archives . . . . . . . . » | 99 |
| Scientific Establishments . . . . . » | 100 |
| Hospitals and Charitable institutions » | 100 |
| Cemitery . . . . . . . . . . » | 101 |
| The Camaldoli . . . . . . . » | 102 |
| Caserta . . . . . . . . . . » | 103 |
| Vesuvius . . . . . . . . . . » | 104 |
| Castellammare . . . . . . . . » | 105 |
| Sorrento . . . . . . . . . . » | 107 |
| Island of Capri . . . . . . . . » | 109 |
| Grotta Azzurra . . . . . . . . » | 110 |
| Poestum . . . . . . . . . . » | 111 |
| Salerno . . . . . . . . . . » | 111 |
| La Cava . . . . . . . . . . » | 113 |
| **Fourth Part**—Addresses . . . . » | 113 |

www.ingramcontent.com/pod-product-compliance
Lightning Source LLC
Chambersburg PA
CBHW022137160426
43197CB00009B/1327